The Lord's supper

A. P. Gibbs

ECS
MINISTRIES
The Word to the World

Books written by Alfred P. Gibbs
Available from ECS Ministries

Christian Baptism
A Dreamer and His Dream
God's Good News
Introduction to a Study of Church Truth
The Lord's Supper
Through the Scriptures
Worship: The Christian's Highest Occupation

The Lord's Supper
Alfred P. Gibbs
Published by:
ECS Ministries
PO Box 1028
Dubuque, IA 52004-1028
phone: (563) 585-2070
email: ecsorders@ecsministries.org
website: www.ecsministries.org
ISBN 978-1-59387-106-2
Code: W-TLS

Previously published by Walterick Publishers.

All Scripture quotations, unless otherwise indicated, are taken from the King James Version. Scripture marked R.V. indicates Revised Version.

Printed in the United States of America

Contents

Analysis of the Lord's Supper

(Referenced by Chapters and Page Numbers)

Foreword

It is indeed a privilege to write this foreword to the latest volume to come from the pen of my beloved brother and valued friend, Alfred P. Gibbs. His book, *Worship,* covers that so important subject in a truly comprehensive manner, and has been a great blessing to my soul in its unfolding of, and stimulus to, the adoration of Him who is worthy of all glory and praise. This book, on the Lord's supper, is a worthy companion volume of that on worship.

I have read the manuscript with deepest interest and delight, and am sure this book ought to have a place on every Christian's bookshelf. The subject itself is unique, for I am not aware of another book devoted entirely to this subject. And it is surely a most important theme. There were *many* forms and ceremonies in Israel; there is only *One* for the Church—the Lord's supper. (Baptism is an individual act). The Lord's supper is the only physical, visible ordinance celebrated by the Church of God in its corporate capacity, when meeting together in Christian fellowship; and therefore it is of the most vital importance. It is *the* witness to the world—a witness men can *see*—of the oneness of the people of God—the fact that the Church is His body.

It is also, and primarily so, the one physical, visible reminder that Christ died, that He shed His precious blood for the salvation of souls. To the believer its blessed merit lies in the fact that it brings back to his mind, each Lord's day, the infinite cost by which he has been redeemed, and reminds him again of the matchless love that brought his Saviour from the throne to the cross.

The chapter devoted to the distinction between the Lord's table and the Lord's supper is especially excellent. I pray that those who do not now remember the Lord Jesus in His precious death by partaking of the Lord's supper every Lord's day may be stirred by this book to do so. And I am sure that those of us who do remember Him thus will find real help and wise advice for its celebration in this book. May the Lord richly use it for His glory and for the refreshment of His dear saints.

–August Van Ryn

Introduction

Our Lord left but two ordinances to be observed by His disciples: Baptism and the Lord's Supper. Others have suggested Biblical precedent for additional practices or "Sacraments." However, careful inductive search of the Word of God solely reveals these two decrees.

The test of the scriptural validity of a Christian ordinance consists of an affirmative answer to three questions asked concerning it. First, was it *commanded* by the Lord Jesus, as recorded in the four Gospels? Second, was it *practiced* in the early Church, as described in the Acts of the Apostles? Third, is its spiritual significance clearly *expounded* in the Epistles? Only two ordinances meet this three fold requirement: Baptism and the Lord's Supper.

The word "sacrament" is not found in the Bible. It is derived from a Latin word, "sacramentum." This word was used in the days of the Roman empire to describe the oath of allegiance which a person took when he joined the army of the Roman empire. In taking this oath, the recruit solemnly vowed that he now renounced his civilian life, with its independence and self pleasing, and from henceforth confessed that he belonged wholly to Caesar, whose every command he promised to obey, cost what it might and lead where it would.

In the early days of Christianity the word came to be used of the two ordinances, Baptism and the Lord's Supper, and for a very good reason. Just as the Roman soldier's "sacramentum" was the act by which he publicly renounced his former life as an independent citizen, to that of a life of loyal and sacrificial service to his Emperor; so a Christian, in those days, by submitting to the ordinance of baptism, and his regular observance of the Lord's supper, proclaimed to the world he had renounced his former life of living for sin and self, and now belonged, body, soul and spirit, to Christ, whom he now boldly owned as the supreme Lord of his life and the sole Master of his service. The observance of these two ordinances thus served the purpose of distinguishing the Christian from the worldling, hence they were called "sacraments."

This explains the fact that even today, in the foreign mission field, and particularly in Moslem countries, a person who professes faith in Christ is not subjected to intense persecution until he has been baptized. This, as it were, becomes his "sacramentum," by which he publicly confesses he has forever renounced the religion of Islam, and now acknowledges Christ as his personal Saviour and Lord. Many such, after their baptism, have been martyred for their testimony.

The New Testament reveals that baptism, which is observed but once, is by immersion in water, and is only intended for those who have professed faith in the Lord Jesus Christ. It is the God-given figure, or illustration, of each Christian's identification with Christ in His death, burial and resurrection. The believer's obedience to this ordinance constitutes his public confession of this fact to others. By submitting to baptism he announces, as it were, to those who witness it: "I hereby confess, in this my baptism, my personal faith in the Person and the substitutionary work of my Lord and Savior, Jesus Christ. I believe that He died for my sins, was buried and rose again for my justification. By my act of obedience to His command I now show forth, in picture, my identification with the Lord Jesus in His death, burial and resurrection. From henceforth, I shall seek to walk in newness of life, and live to the glory of the One 'who loved me and gave Himself for me.'" (Read Matt. 28:19-20; Acts 8:26-39; Rom. 6:3-6.)

The New Testament also reveals that the Lord's supper, which is to be observed frequently, is only for those who have been saved by the grace of God. This ordinance consists of believers meeting together, in the name of the Lord Jesus, and breaking and partaking of a loaf of bread, picture of the body of Christ, and drinking of a cup containing the fruit of the vine, symbol of the precious blood of Christ, by which their eternal redemption has been secured.

Thus the Lord's supper is a simple memorial ordinance which was given by the Savior on the night of His betrayal. It exists only for the purpose of enabling His disciples to gratefully remember Him as they take the bread and drink the wine, and thus show forth His death until He returns for them. (Read Matt. 26:26-29; Mark 14:22-26; Acts 20:7; 1 Cor. 11:23-34.)

In spite of the plain directions found in the Word of God, Christendom, through the years, by its many additions, subtractions and human inventions, has perverted each of these beautiful ordinances. Instead of baptism being the divinely ordained picture of a work of regeneration already accomplished in the *experience* of the believer, it is now declared to be the *means* by which this regeneration is to be accomplished! Thus baptism has been endowed with a magical and saving quality.

Moreover, in many cases, the sprinkling of infants, which the Bible knows nothing about, has been substituted for the immersion of professed believers. In both the Roman Catholic and in many Protestant denominations, it is actually affirmed that a baby, at its christening, is made "a member of Christ, a child of God and an inheritor of the kingdom of God!" Thus, what was originally intended to *illustrate* the believer's identification with Christ, is now declared to be the *means* of this identification! The symbol has been allowed to become the *substitute* for salvation, and the ordinance has been permitted to displace the Savior Himself.

The same has become true of the Lord's supper. It has been allowed to degenerate from a simple memorial and remembrance feast for regenerated believers into the sacrifice of the Mass. To the accompaniment of a host of prescribed prayers and an ornate ritual, in which gorgeous vestments, burning candles, smoking incense, an altar and many crosses play no small part, the bread and wine is said to be miraculously changed into the literal body and blood of Christ! These practices, at the very minimum, alter the Lord's original intent and meaning of the His Supper.

History, as we all know, has a bad habit of repeating itself. The Lord Jesus found similar conditions prevailing when He became incarnate and lived on earth. The religious leaders of the people of Israel, the Pharisees, had permitted a host of traditions to supercede the authority of the holy Scriptures. The "Feasts of Jehovah," as given by God to Israel had, in a thousand years, degenerated into "feasts of the Jews." (See Lev. 23; John 5:1, 6:4.) Our Lord fearlessly rebuked these religious leaders for this sin of perverting the Word of God by their traditions and said: "Why do ye also transgress the commandment of God by your tradition? . . . Ye have made the commandment of God of none effect by your tradition. . . . In vain do they worship Me, teaching for doctrines the commandments of men" (Matt. 15:1-9; Mark 7:1-13).

In the pages that follow, we shall seek to deal particularly with the ordinance of the Lord's supper, and endeavor to discover something of its great importance and deep spiritual significance to every true Christian. We are exhorted in the Scriptures to: "Sanctify the Lord God in your hearts: and be ready always to give an answer to every man that asketh you a reason of the hope that is within you with meekness and fear" (1 Peter 3:15).

Every Christian, therefore, should be prepared, when asked, to turn to the Word of God and give a scriptural reason for his observance of the Lord's supper. It is to be feared that many, particularly the children of Christian parents, who are familiar, from childhood, with the scriptural observance of this ordinance, and perhaps partake of the Lord's supper themselves, would be at a loss to give such a scriptural answer.

It will be recalled that when God instituted the feast of the Passover, He made allowance for the natural curiosity of children, for we read: "And ye shall observe this thing for an ordinance to thee and to thy sons for ever. And it shall come to pass, when ye be come to the land which the Lord will give you, according as He hath promised, that ye shall keep this service. And it shall come to pass when your children shall say unto you, 'What mean ye by this service?' That ye shall say, 'It is the sacrifice of the Lord's passover, who passed over the houses of the children of Israel in Egypt, when He smote the Egyptians, and delivered our houses'" (Ex. 12:24-26). The same is also true of the instructions given regarding the redemption of the firstling of a donkey by means of the death of a lamb, and the memorial stones from the river Jordan (Ex. 13:13-15; Josh. 4:4-9).

Similarly, every Christian who observes the Lord's supper should be prepared to answer any person who asks: "What mean ye by this service?" He should be able to turn to the various passages of Scripture which speak of its institution by the Lord Jesus, the purpose for which it was given, the spiritual significance of the bread and the cup, the condition necessary for partaking of it, and the glorious event to which it points forward.

Surely such an ordinance, instituted by the Son of God on the eve of His substitutionary sacrifice, should merit the earnest consideration of all true Christians. Our Savior's words: "This do for a remembrance of Me," should demand the attention of all who profess to be His disciples, and lead them to take their place, each Lord's day, with the Lord's people, in the way that He appointed.

May it be our goal, as we search the Scriptures, to come to a better understanding of the spiritual significance of this blessed ordinance, and therefore more deeply appreciate both the privilege and the responsibility of observing it in a scriptural manner, apart from the confusion that prevails in Christendom. If the reading of these pages shall lead to this result, then the effort of writing on this subject will be more than amply repaid.

We shall think of our subject under several main divisions as follows:

I. Some suppers of the New Testament

II. The distinction between the Lord's Table and the Lord's Supper

III. The institution of the Lord's Supper

IV. The symbolism of the Lord's Supper

V. The purpose of the Lord's Supper

VI. The participants of the Lord's Supper

VII. The procedure of the Lord's Supper

VIII. The day and frequency of the Lord's Supper

IX. The Christian's responsibility to the Lord's Supper

X. A summary of the Lord's Supper

A detailed analysis will be found following the list of contents, which will enable the reader to grasp the subject as a whole, and also enable him to refer quickly to any particular part in which he is interested.

My very good friend and beloved brother in Christ, Mr. August Van Ryn, of Hialeah, Florida, the well known and highly esteemed teacher of the Word, and author of many excellent books on Scripture subjects, has kindly read the manuscript and written a Foreword to this book, for which I am very grateful.

My thanks are also due to Mr. Frank Biffen, of Lake Worth, Florida, for his kindness in correcting the manuscript, and for many valuable suggestions in regard to its composition.

Chapter One

Suppers of the New Testament

Many suppers are described in the New Testament, and each one has its own particular spiritual significance to the believer. Let us take a brief look at seven of these.

The Supper of the Gospel Proclamation
(Luke 14:16-24)

From this parable we learn that God has provided a great supper, and has commissioned His servants to issue the invitation: "Come, for all things are now ready." Those who excused themselves from attending were taken at their word and excused. The poor, maimed, halt and blind, together with the friendless and the outcast, were welcomed to the sumptuous repast. Each time the gospel is proclaimed, the invitation is extended to "whosoever will"; and all who respond and believe on the Son of God are pardoned, cleansed and relieved. Happy indeed are those who have owned their guilt as lost, helpless and hopeless sinners, and have rested in the merits of the substitutionary sacrifice of the Lord Jesus, trusted Him as their own personal Savior and confessed Him as the Lord of their lives. Such can joyously testify:

> Nought have I gotten, but what I received,
> Grace hath bestowed it since I have believed;
> Boasting excluded, pride I abase:
> I'm only a sinner saved by grace!

The Supper of Spiritual Fellowship
(Rev. 3:20)

This is the supper which the Lord of glory desires to enjoy with each believer who will respond to His gracious invitation, and allow Him to enter into his life as his supreme Lord, and thus give Him the place of absolute preeminence in every department of his being. Christ will then sup with him and he, in turn, will sup with the Lord, and thus enjoy the sweet communion that only the Son of God can make possible. Christ will then become to him:

> A living, bright reality,
> More present to faith's vision keen,
> Than any earthly object seen;
> More dear, more intimately nigh,
> Than e'en the closest earthly tie.
> (F. R. Havergal)

The Supper of the Believer's Appreciation
(John 12:1-8)

Out of the love and deep appreciation of their hearts, a few friends of the Lord made Him a supper. Though the Lord came as the Guest of honor, in reality He was the Host. What joy these dear friends of His brought to His heart when, "six days before the Passover," they expressed their love for Him by spreading the table in His honor, and ministering to His needs! It will be recalled that it was on this occasion that Mary took the costly perfume and anointed the feet of her Lord, and then wiped His feet with her hair, so that the whole house was filled with the exquisite fragrance of the spikenard. What an unspeakable honor was theirs, that day, in being privileged to entertain the King of kings and the Lord of lords!

The Supper of Typical Consummation
(Luke 22:7-18)

This was the purpose for which the Passover feast had been instituted hundreds of years before. Its real spiritual meaning was now to be explained and fulfilled. The countless lambs, which had been sacrificed upon the altars of Jewry, had all pointed forward to this night of nights. Christ, the eternal Son of God, was about to offer Himself, without spot to God, as a substitutionary sacrifice for our sins, and thus make possible the salvation of all who would rest in His finished work, trust Him as Savior and own Him as Lord.

It was the last Passover supper that had any value in the sight of God, for there was to be no need of any more. All who now shelter behind the efficacy of the precious blood of Christ have the glad assurance from the God of all grace: "When I see the blood, I will pass over you!" (Ex. 12:1-15). They can therefore sing with glad accord:

No blood, no altar now,
  The sacrifice is o'er
No flame, no smoke ascends on high,
  The lamb is slain no more.
But richer blood has flowed from nobler veins,
  To purge the soul from guilt,
And cleanse the reddest stains!

(H. Bonar)

The Supper of Nuptial Celebration
(Rev. 19:9)

The Church, the espoused bride of Christ, is now to become the Bride of the Lamb, and the invitation is extended to attend the marriage supper. No wonder, therefore, that we read: "Blessed are they which are called to the marriage supper of the Lamb!" He who "loved the Church and gave Himself for it," is now to celebrate the union of Himself with His blood-bought Bride. What a supper this shall be! There will be no denominational distinctions at this supper! No special section reserved for this sect or that party! All the artificial barriers that separate the people of God today will be done away with for ever—good riddance to bad rubbish! Our Lord's prayer, as recorded in John 17, will then be fully answered: "That they all may be one, as Thou, Father, art in Me, and I in Thee, that they also may be one in Us." The Church, in that day, shall be presented by the Lord to Himself, "a glorious Church, without spot or wrinkle, or any such thing, but that it should be holy and without blemish." (Eph. 5: 27)

The Supper of Just Retribution
(Rev. 19:17)

To this supper, the fowls of the air are invited to feed upon the bodies of those slain by the avenging Judge of all the earth. It is called, "the great supper of God." (RV). Here the Lord is described as doing His "strange work," the work of just retribution upon the wilfully impenitent. Here the worldly great, in all their majesty, pride, pomp and power, are brought down into the dust of death by the omnipotent Son of God, to whom all judgment has been committed. Note the title He is given in this connection: "The Faithful and True . . . the Word of God." (vs. 11-13)

Happy are they who have bowed the knee to Him in time, and have gladly owned Him as their Lord and Savior! Those who die in their sins will be compelled in this day, to bow the knee to Him and confess that "Jesus Christ is Lord, to the glory of God the Father." (Phil. 2:9-11)

The Supper of Grateful Remembrance
(1 Cor. 11:17-34)

This supper is distinguished from all these other suppers by the title: "The Lord's Supper." It is the supper that Christ Himself instituted for His people in order to give them the opportunity of expressing to Him their gratitude, praise, worship and adoration for all that He is in His divine person, and all that He has done in His sacrifice on their behalf. This is the supper which will occupy our attention for the remaining pages of this book.

Chapter Two

The Distinction Between the Lord's Table and the Lord's Supper

Before going into detail regarding the Lord's supper, it may be well to examine the distinction that exists between the terms: "The Lord's table," as described in 1 Corinthians 10; and "The Lord's supper," as outlined in 1 Corinthians 11. Though these terms have certain things in common, yet they are distinct in thought. The very fact that the Spirit of God uses these two different terms surely means that He wishes to impress us with two different things. In our study of the Bible, we are exhorted to "prove (or distinguish) the things that differ" (Phil. 1:10 RV).

Let us consider, first of all, the things that they have in common. First, both are described as being the Lord's, thus indicating they have a common ownership. Next, each views the people of God as being partakers of its provision. Then again, both speak of the bread and the cup. Finally, each is viewed as conferring a privilege, and demanding a corresponding responsibility. It is because they have these things in common that many look upon the Lord's table and the Lord's supper as being synonymous terms. However, as we examine them more closely, we shall discover that though they are related, yet there is a marked distinction between them. Let us note some of these distinctions.

1. There is a distinction in the terms used: "table" and "supper." If words mean anything, then there is surely a difference between a table and a supper. A well known teacher has aptly observed: "If the Lord uses a different word in connection with a matter, then He wrote to convey to us a different idea; and although one may, in a measure, be incorporated in the other the variation has some difference of meaning" (Alfred Mace).

2. The term, "The Lord's table," is common to both the Old and the New Testament; whereas "the Lord's supper" is only used in the New Testament. Malachi uses the word "table" as being synonymous with the altar, from which God supplied the needs of the priests. (See Lev. 6:16, 26; 7:6, 31-32; Num. 18:21, 24, 30; cp. 1 Cor. 9:13, 10:18; Mal. 1:7.) Note Malachi's words: "Ye offer polluted bread upon Mine altar, and ye say

'Wherein have we polluted Thee?' In that ye say, 'The table of the Lord is contemptible.'" Again, in verse 12, he says: "But ye have profaned it, in that ye say: 'The table of the Lord is polluted, and the fruit thereof, even His meat is contemptible.'" (See also Ezek. 41:22.)

The altar was literally the table of the Lord from which the priest derived his physical nourishment. A certain part of the sacrifices brought to the altar become the portion of the priest (Josh. 13:14). Thus the altar became his "table," by which his physical needs were met. If the people of Israel were lax in bringing their offerings, the priest suffered as a result. In this way the "altar" became his "table." It was God's way of providing for the needs of the priests. (See Ex. 23:18; Lev. 21:6; Num. 28:2; etc.)

By the word, "table," therefore, is meant the *provision* of the Lord for His people. Needless to say, it is not a *literal* table that is in view, but a *figurative* one. The term simply stands for the provision it supplies. For instance, it has often been said of a lady who has a boarding house that "she keeps a good table." By this is not meant the literal wooden table, as a piece of furniture, but the quality and quantity of the food she supplies to her guests.

David spoke of this table when he said: "Thou preparest a table before me in the presence of mine enemies." (Ps. 23:5) Did he refer to a literal table, with four legs and made of wood? Of course not. He was speaking of the Lord's provision for all his needs. Israel, in their unbelief, inquired: "Can God furnish a table in the wilderness?" The answer, in the affirmative, is seen in God's provision of the manna from heaven and the water from the rock of flint (Ps. 78:19; Deut. 8:3, 15). In Proverbs 9:2 we read that wisdom has "furnished her table." David prayed that the table of his enemies would become "a snare before them" (Ps. 69:22). We read of "the prophets of the groves which eat at Jezebel's table" (1 Kings 18:19). In other words, they partook of her provision. Thus the "table" speaks of provision. By the term: "The Lord's table" is meant the sum total of all God's provision for His people, and this, of course, would also include the Lord's supper. Thus "the Lord's table" is a *general* and *inclusive* term.

The term, "the Lord's supper," is used only in the New Testament, and is exclusively an ordinance for Christians only. It belongs to the dispensation of the Church, the called out company of those redeemed by the precious blood of Christ, regenerated by the Holy Spirit and united to Christ, the

Head, in heaven, and to every other believer on earth. "The Lord's Supper" is therefore, a *specific* and *exclusive* term that refers to one thing only.

3. There is a difference in the context, or the subject matter in which the words are found. In the case of the Lord's table, the prominent thought is *fellowship.* Notice the words: "communion," "partakers," "fellowship." (1 Cor. 10:16-18, 20-21, 30.) At the Lord's table we express the fact that we have died with Christ, and henceforth are identified with Him at His table. Here the believer is seen in *contrast to the world.*

At the Lord's supper, the prominent thought is *remembrance* and *proclamation* (1 Cor. 11:24-26). There is no mention of communion. At the supper, we express the fact that Christ died for us, for we "proclaim the Lord's death, till He come," each time we observe this ordinance. Thus, at the supper, the believer is seen in *relation to the assembly.*

4. There is no mention of a "coming together" at the Lord's table, for all the Lord's people are viewed as being already together and partaking of the Lord's provision at His table. No believer has even to take a physical step to get to the Lord's table, for he is described as being *already there,* enjoying the rich provision of God's infinite grace.

At the Lord's supper, however, there is a "coming together," on the part of the Lord's people, to observe this ordinance. See 1 Corinthians 11:18, 20. Our Lord declared: "Where two or three are gathered together in My Name, there am I in the midst of them" (Matt. 18:20). This coming together therefore demands a deliberate and physical act on the part of each believer.

5. The Lord's table is viewed in contrast to two other tables: the table of Israel (1 Cor. 10:18, cp. Mal. 1:12), and the table of demons for idolaters (1 Cor. 10:20-21). A failure to appreciate this distinction between the table and the supper has led some over zealous brethren to make the unjust and entirely erroneous assertion that the celebration of the Lord's supper amongst the denominations was, in reality, a partaking of the table of demons!

The Lord's supper, on the contrary, is not viewed in contrast with anything else. Like Christianity itself, it is unique and stands alone, as a memorial to the Founder of Christianity, who made it possible at the infinite cost of His precious blood.

6. All believers are viewed as being participants and partakers of the provision of the Lord's table. "We, being many are one bread, and one body" (1 Cor. 10:17). The moment a person is saved, he is viewed, by God, as being at the Lord's table. At this table he remains all the days of his Christian life. An illustration of this can be seen in the case of Mephibosheth. When he was brought into the presence and favor of David, we are told "he did eat continually at the king's table" (2 Sam. 9:13). This does not mean that he spent every moment of his time eating at David's table, but that David's provision was continually at his disposal, and that David's table was his rightful place and privilege.

In 1 Corinthians 5:8, the *whole period* of the believer's life is likened to the feast of unleavened bread, which was associated with the feast of the Passover. The Lord's table is a *permanent* thing, from which the believer is never absent. Every moment of every day and night he is viewed by God as being there.

In contrast to this, Christians are not always viewed as being at the Lord's supper, for it is written: "As *often* as ye eat this bread and drink this cup, ye do shew the Lord's death till He come" (1 Cor. 11:26). From Acts 20:7 we learn that this took place on the first day of the week. Thousands of truly saved children, all of whom are at the Lord's table, have not yet partaken of the Lord's supper, and will not do so until they have seen their privilege and responded to His request: "This do for a remembrance of Me." Then again, there are many born again believers in the Salvation Army who have never partaken of the elements, as also many of the Society of Friends, who do not believe that the Lord's supper is a literal one, but believe it is a spiritual communion in the sense of Revelation 3:20.

All saved persons, irrespective of their obedience to the Lord in baptism or the Lord's supper, are described as being at the Lord's table. Many Christians, through sickness, untoward circumstances, or apathy, are not always in their place at the Lord's supper, but they are never absent from the Lord's table. The Lord's table is a *permanent* thing, but the Lord's supper is only a *temporary* thing, for at the Lord's coming it will cease to exist.

7. The Lord's table is not visible to human eyes. It cannot be seen, smelled, tasted or touched. It is a spiritual reality nevertheless and, as we have seen, is figurative of the sum total of all God's provision for His people.

The Lord's supper is something that can be seen, smelled, tasted and touched. There is a loaf of bread and a cup containing the fruit of the vine. It is a literal loaf and a literal cup that symbolizes the body and blood of the Lord. The table on which the bread and cup is placed is not the Lord's table, it is simply a piece of furniture which conveniently holds the elements. A box, or even the floor would serve the same purpose. A lady, writing to a friend, bemoaned the fact that, during the meeting, "one of the legs of the Lord's table had collapsed!" Another brother declared very emphatically he would never partake of the Lord's supper at a certain Summer Bible conference, "because they had moved the Lord's table from a certain city to that Bible conference!" One thing is certain, no one has ever seen, much less moved the Lord's table from one place to another. The Lord's supper, however, may be observed in one place this Lord's day and in another place the following week.

8. The Lord's table is not a rite, nor an ordinance to be observed, but a provision that has been supplied by the Lord for all His people. The Lord's supper is an ordinance, instituted by the Lord Himself on the night of His betrayal, and is to be observed by Christians as an act of obedience. Not only so, but the Lord's supper is the subject of a special revelation from the glorified Lord to His servant, Paul (1 Cor. 11:23). Our Lord's request demands a voluntary and willing act of obedience on the part of each participant.

9. The Lord's table is a provision spread by God for the benefit of His people. Like Solomon's table of long ago, it has an exceedingly abundant supply, and is more than adequate to meet every need that can possibly arise in the experience of every believer (1 Kings 4:22-23). It was this munificent display of food that so impressed the queen of Sheba, for we are told she saw "the meat of his table, and the sitting of his servants, and the attendance of his ministers and their apparel, and his cupbearers" (1 Kings 10:5). If this sight of Solomon's table aroused her wonder and praise, what shall be said of the Lord's table, as we contemplate the superabundant supply of the exceeding riches of His grace!

The Lord's supper, however, is one that we *spread for the Lord* in order to do Him honor. At His request, Christians gladly come together in a certain place and spread a table for Him. They provide the loaf of bread and the cup of wine, together with seats for the believers who attend, and thus in this simple, but scriptural fashion, remember the Lord Jesus in the way He appointed. At the Lord's table we *receive from Him*, but at the Lord's supper *He receives from us!*

10. No human being or any company of human beings, can either receive to, or put away a person from the Lord's table. This is the sole prerogative of the Lord Himself, and He has assured us that "him that cometh unto Me, I will in no wise cast out" (John 6:37). The Lord calls, receives, saves and eternally keeps all His own. In this, He is absolutely sovereign, and no one and no thing can ever thwart His gracious and eternal purpose.

At the Lord's supper, however, Christians may welcome their fellow believers, if they are sound in doctrine and moral in life. They are also given authority, if the circumstances should warrant it, to put away a person from their gathering and deny him the right to partake of the Lord's supper. (See 1 Cor. 5:11-13; Rom. 15:7.) Thus, in the Lord's supper there is the element of human responsibility.

11. In the description of the Lord's table, the cup, which symbolizes the blood of Christ, is mentioned first, and the bread, which speaks of His body, is mentioned last (1 Cor. 10:16). In the Lord's supper, the bread is mentioned first and then the cup. Why is the order reversed? The answer is simple. It is the precious blood of Christ that makes possible our place at the Lord's table. Apart from the substitutionary sacrifice of Christ, which necessitated the shedding of His blood, there could neither be the remission of sins, nor the provision of the Lord's table. We need ever to remind ourselves that: "We were not redeemed with corruptible things, as silver and gold . . . but with the precious blood of Christ, as of a Lamb without blemish and without spot" (1 Peter 1:18-19).

In the Lord's supper, as ordained by the Lord Himself, the order is, first the bread and then the cup; for this is an ordinance by which we remember the One who gave Himself for us. Thus, we take the bread, emblem of His body in the which He bore our sins, and this focuses our minds on His Person. Then we take the cup, and thus are brought to realize the awful cost, to Him, of our eternal redemption.

12. In the description of the Lord's table, the bread is said to be a picture of the mystical body of Christ, the Church, formed by the Holy Spirit on the day of Pentecost. We are told: "For by (in) one Spirit are we all baptized into one body . . . and have all been made to drink into one Spirit" (1 Cor. 12:13). Thus the bread here symbolizes the unity of all believers, hence it says: "For we, being many are one bread and one body: for we are all partakers of that one bread" (1 Cor. 10:17). Thus the bread, at the Lord's table, represents the sum total of all believers.

At the Lord's supper, the bread is distinctly declared to be a picture or the symbol of the a*ctual body of our Lord,* in the which He wrought our redemption. This explains why the Corinthian believers had come under the chastening hand of God, for they had been observing the Lord's supper in an unworthy manner, and had not been "discerning the Lord's body" (1 Cor. 11:29).

13. In the description of the Lord's table, the partaking of the cup and bread is called a "communion" with His death (1 Cor. 10:16-17). In the Lord's supper, the partaking of the elements is said to be a *proclamation* of His death (1 Cor. 11:26).

14. In connection with the Lord's table, the partakers are warned about living unworthily (1 Cor. 10:21). In the Lord's supper the warning is directed against *eating unworthily* (1 Cor. 11:29).

15. At the Lord's table, there is no mention of the Lord's second coming, for believers will always be at the Lord's table. At death, the believer does not cease to be a partaker of the provision of the Lord's table. In fact, he is declared to be "with Christ, which is far better" (Phil. 1:23).

The Lord's supper, however, is only to be observed "until He come" (1 Cor. 11:26). At Christ's coming, there will be no more need for the Lord's supper. We shall no longer require the bread and the cup to remind us of His body and blood for, with glorified bodies, we shall be forever with and like Him. What a glorious prospect is ours!

Thus we have seen that the Lord's table and the Lord's supper, though related, are quite distinct, and each believer would do well to keep these distinctions in mind, It will be recalled that Paul's desire for the believers at Philippi was that they might learn to "try [distinguish] the things that differ" Phil. 1:10 (marg.).

Chapter Three

The Institution of the Lord's Supper:
Person, Circumstances, Passover

For this we have abundant Scriptural evidence. Both Matthew, Mark and Luke describe the event. (See Matt. 26:26-29; Mark 14:22-26; Luke 22:19-20.) The apostle Paul, who was not present at its institution, was given a special revelation concerning it by none other than the Lord Himself. Let us look at his words: "For I have received of the Lord that which I also delivered unto you, that the Lord Jesus, the same night in which He was betrayed, took bread: And when He had given thanks, He brake it, and said, 'Take, eat: this is My body, which is broken for you: this do in remembrance of Me.' After the same manner also He took the cup, when He had supped, saying, 'This cup is the new testament in My blood: this do ye, as oft as ye drink it, in remembrance of Me.' For as often as ye eat this bread and drink this cup, ye do show the Lord's death till He come" (1 Cor. 11:23-26).

Thus we have four accounts of the institution of this divinely appointed ordinance. Let us think of four things in this connection. First, the Person who instituted it. Second, the circumstances of its institution. Third, the Passover. Fourth, the institution of the Lord's supper.

The Person Who Instituted It

Our authority for the observance of this ordinance is the highest possible. It is none other than the eternal Son of the eternal God who, in the infinitude of His grace, clothed Himself with humanity and became Man. In Paul's account of the institution of the supper, the word "Lord" occurs seven times. (See 1 Cor. 11:20, 23, 26-27, 29, 32.) Thus the absolute Lordship of Christ is emphasized, both in the institution and the observance of this ordinance.

We cannot emphasize too strongly the fact that it is the *Lord's supper*. It does not belong to any special group of believers. No denomination has any exclusive rights to its celebration. It is the surpassing dignity of the

Person who instituted it that gives the supper its incomparable virtue and value. He is the central Object, and the sole explanation of its existence. Morover, He is the Host at His own supper, and those present are His very greatly honored and most highly privileged guests. Consequently, we are not told to invite people to this supper, for this is the sole prerogative of the Host Himself. A person, who is a guest in the home of a friend, would not take it upon himself to go around and invite some of his friends to the home of his host. He wisely leaves this matter to his host and hostess. As their guest, he will gladly welcome all whom his host invites to his home. This is exactly the situation in regards to the Lord's supper.

Who can possibly undertake to describe this glorious Being, equal and eternal with the Father and the Holy Spirit, "The only begotten of the Father, full of grace and truth" John 1:14)? He is the One of whom it is said: "God . . . hath in these last days spoken unto us by [in] His Son, whom He hath appointed Heir of all things, by whom also He made the worlds; who, being the brightness of His glory, and the express image (character) of His Person, and upholding all things by the word of His power, when He had by Himself purged our sins, sat down on the right hand of the majesty on high" (Heb. 1:1-3).

We do well to sing:

> Join all the glorious names
> Of wisdom, love and power,
> That mortals ever knew,
> That angels ever bore;
> All are too mean to speak His worth,
> Too mean to set the Savior forth!
> (Isaac Watts)

While it is entirely beyond our natural *comprehension* to grasp all that is involved in the incarnation of the Son of God; yet it is not beyond our spiritual *apprehension*. We believe the record that God has given of His Son (1 John 4:14-15, 5:9-13). This record declares: "In the beginning was the Word, (the Logos), and the Word was with God, and the Word was God" (John 1:1). Here His absolute essential and eternal Deity is set forth in unmistakable language, admitting of no other interpretation. To deny the eternal Sonship of Christ is to deny the eternal Fatherhood of God, for one necessitates the other. How blessed it is to know that the eternal Father sent His eternal Son, who, through the eternal Spirit, offered Himself as a substitutionary sacrifice on our behalf, that we might be redeemed unto God! (Heb. 9:14).

Thus the One who instituted this ordinance was "God manifest in the flesh." He was the One who, "though He was rich, yet for your sakes He became poor, that ye through His poverty might become rich" (1 Tim. 3:16; 2 Cor. 8:9). Once this fundamental truth is grasped, the importance of this supper will become apparent to every believer.

To be invited to the home of a friend who occupies the same station in life as oneself is a common event, but to be invited to the home of the president of a great republic, or to the palace of a king is a different matter entirely. What shall be said of one who is invited to supper by the King of kings and the Lord of lords! C. H. Spurgeon put it beautifully when he wrote:

> What food luxurious loads the board
> When, at His table sits the Lord!
> The wine, how rich, the bread, how sweet,
> When Jesus deigns the guests to meet!

The Circumstances of its Institution

1. The Time

How impressive are the words: "The Lord Jesus, the same night in which He was betrayed, took bread." What a graphic picture is painted for us in these few words! Conceived by the Holy Spirit, and born of a virgin, our Lord had lived for thirty years in the obscure village of Nazareth, where He had worked as a carpenter. At the end of this period He had been baptized by John, and then had entered upon His public ministry. For three and a half years He had travelled through the land of Palestine with His twelve disciples, and had fully demonstrated His deity by the sinless life He lived, the wondrous words He spake, and the mighty miracles He performed.

The popularity that had first attended His ministry quickly waned, and gave place to indifference and hostility and had now ripened into intense hatred on the part of the leaders of the nation of Israel. He had exposed their hypocrisy and plainly and fearlessly denounced their sin. Now, with the connivance of Judas, they are plotting His betrayal and murder. This, then, is the somber setting of the scene.

2. The Place

It was with the full knowledge of all the "things that should come upon Him" (John 18:4) that the Lord gave instructions for the preparation of the Passover meal. Peter and John were commissioned to go into the city of Jerusalem, and the Lord foretold the various incidents that would take place as they entered the city. He described the man with the pitcher of water who should lead them to the house. He instructed them as to what question to put to the good man of the house. He described the kind of room that had been prepared for the feast of the Passover. Thus this *provision* was the evident result of His divine *provision*.

Three things were said of the place where the Lord's supper was to be instituted, and this is redolent with spiritual meaning.

(a) It was to be a large room

It was to be big enough to receive all whom the Lord desired to be with Him. Likewise, at the Lord's supper, there should be room enough for all believers who are sound in doctrine and life, and who desire to remember the Lord. To impose any other conditions is to have too small a room. Mark the words: "Wherefore receive ye one another, as Christ also received us to the glory of God" (Rom. 15:7). Is the assembly of believers with whom you meet prepared to welcome all whom Christ has received? Does it have room for all the truth of the Word of God?

(b) It was an upper room

It was located above the busy bustling crowds that thronged the street beneath. Surely this speaks of what the Lord's supper means to those who gather, in His name, to remember Him. As the poet has put it:

> Shut in with Thee, far, far above
> The restless world that wars below.

Through their great high Priest, believers may enter into the holiest, and know what it means for their souls to be bathed in celestial air (Heb. 10:19-22).

(c) It was a furnished room

All that was necessary for the comfort and convenience of the guests had been supplied. Simplicity and practicability marked the furnishing. No altar, no gorgeous vestments, no incense, no prescribed prayers, no crosses and no "officiating clergyman." What a pleasant contrast to the elaborate ritual, performed in huge and imposing buildings, that we see in Christendom today! All that is needed for the observance of the Lord's supper is a loaf of bread and a cup containing the fruit of the vine. With Christ in their midst, the word of God in their hands, and the Holy Spirit in their hearts, what more can believers possibly need for the remembrance of their Lord and Savior?

The Passover

Mark the words of the Savior as He sat with His disciples, "With desire have I desired to eat this Passover with you before I suffer" (Luke 22:16). The word means "earnestly desire." This was the Passover He had in mind when, hundreds of years before, He had given instructions to Israel, through Moses, to observe it (Ex. 12:1-14). We need ever to keep in mind that the "Jehovah" of the Old Testament is the "Jesus" of the New Testament. All that is predicated of Jehovah in the Old is claimed, by the Lord Jesus, in the New. The countless thousands of lambs, which had been sacrificed since the inception of the Passover, had all pointed forward to this particular night when the Lamb of God was about to offer Himself as a sacrifice to God on behalf of our sins. Truly, it was the night of nights, when all the types of the Old Testament were about to be fulfilled, and the old dispensation of the Law was to give place to the glad dispensation of Grace.

Little did the people of Jerusalem realize, as they passed by that upper room, what tremendous things were taking place within its walls! The Passover that was to end all Passovers was being celebrated! All succeeding Passovers would be utterly meaningless and valueless in the eyes of God, for we read: "Christ, our Passover, is sacrificed for us" (1 Cor. 5:7). The old covenant was about to give place to the new covenant which was soon to be signed, sealed and ratified by the death and resurrection of our Lord Jesus Christ. The time had come when Christ was about to offer "the one sacrifice for sins for ever" (Heb. 10:12), by which He was to satisfy all the demands of a holy law and the righteous claims of Divine justice.

What tremendous meaning is enshrined in the words: "Then came the day of unleavened bread when the Passover *must* be killed" (Luke 22:7). This statement should be interpreted in the light of our Savior's words to Nicodemus: "As Moses lifted up the serpent in the wilderness, even so *must* the Son of Man be lifted up" (John 3:14). Since the sinner *must* be born again if he would ever see or enter the kingdom of God, then the Savior *must* be lifted up to make such a regeneration possible, for, "without the shedding of blood, there is no remission" (Heb. 9:22).

The Passover presents a beautiful picture of God's way of salvation today. On the night of the Passover, there was but *one way of salvation*—a lamb slain. There was but *one ground of assurance*—the promise of God's word: "When I see the blood, I will pass over you." There was but *one place of safety*—behind the blood applied to the doorpost of the house. Our Lord well knew, on this fateful night, that He was soon to fulfill the type of the spotless lamb that was slain. He well knew that, consequent upon His death and resurrection, thousands upon thousands of sinners would be saved by trusting in the merits of His shed blood, assured of their salvation by His own precious word, and kept by His mighty power.

With these thoughts in our minds, we can appreciate the meaning of those simple words: "When the hour was come, He sat down and the twelve apostles with Him" (Luke 22:14). It is difficult to discover just what was the exact order of events at this Passover supper, for Luke does not give us the chronological order. Edersheim, in his monumental work, *The Life and Times of Jesus the Messiah*, gives us some interesting details as to how the Passover feast was conducted during those days, and the reader would be well advised to get a copy of this classic on the life of Christ. He suggests the following sequence of events.

1. The discussion among the apostles as to who was the greatest (Luke 22:24-30)

In the light of these circumstances, this seems almost incredible. In the shadow of the cross they discussed the matter of leadership amongst them! How little they had learned from their Master who, both by precept and example, had demonstrated that He was "meek and lowly in heart" (Matt. 11:29).

Perhaps the question was raised in order to determine how they should sit, or recline at the table with Him. It is a sad commentary on human nature, and on the utter unprofitableness of the flesh that, on this intensely solemn occasion, there should have been any thought of precedence among them. The Lord's rebuke: "He that is greatest among you, let him be as the younger, and he that is chief, as he that doth serve," would surely put them to shame. Doubtless it was with red faces that they took their places at the table. This table was usually rectangular in shape, and couches were arranged around three sides of it in the shape of an elongated horseshoe.

2. Thanksgiving for the first cup (Luke 22:17)

Altogether three cups were used at the feast. The usual formula, as the first cup was taken, was for the host to say: "Blessed art Thou, Jehovah our God, who hath created the fruit of the vine." The cup was then passed to all present.

3. The washing of the disciples' feet (John 13:2-12)

Note the Revised Version wording, "During supper." According to the usual observance of the Passover, the next thing was for the host to rise and wash his hands. Instead, to the astonishment of the disciples, they saw their Lord arise, lay aside His garments, take a towel, gird Himself, pour water into a basin and begin to wash His disciples feet, and wipe them with the towel. Thus the Lord exemplified, by His actions, what He had expressed with His lips. In this way, the Lord altered the regular order of the Passover, for He was the Lord of the Passover, as He was the Lord of the Sabbath, and everything else in His creation.

To Peter's objection: "Lord, dost Thou wash my feet?" our Lord's answer is full of spiritual import: "What I do now, thou knowest not, but thou shalt know hereafter." He then proceeded to impress upon their hearts the difference between the complete bathing of regeneration which is *once for all*, and never repeated, and the constant need for the *daily cleansing* of the feet from the defilement of the world. Thus He taught that *regeneration* is one thing, and *fellowship* is another. There can be no fellowship without regeneration, but there may be regeneration without fellowship.

Many artists have tried to picture the scene: the Lord of life and glory kneeling at the travel-stained feet of His disciples, and performing the service of a lowly servant. How blessed it is to know that He who *made* us "clean, every whit," by His substitutionary sacrifice, now ever lives, as our Advocate and great high Priest, to *keep* us clean, so that one day He will "present us to Himself without spot or wrinkle, or any such thing" (Eph. 5:27). May it be ours to come constantly to the water of the Word of God, and so apply its truth to our lives, that we shall be kept clean and useful to our Lord and Savior! (Eph. 5:26).

4. The continuation of the Passover supper (John 13:12)

After the Lord had resumed His place at the table, He proceeded to apply the truth which He had demonstrated by His example. Note how He reversed the order of His titles: "Ye call Me Master and Lord, and ye say well, for so I am. If I then, your Lord and Master, have washed your feet, ye ought also to wash one another's feet." In these words He indicated that it is possible for Christ to be the Master of our service without necessarily being the Lord of our life; but He cannot be the Lord of our life without also being the Master of all our service. (See 1 Peter 3:15 R.V.) It will be noticed that Judas called Him "Master," but did not address Him as "Lord" (Matt. 26:25). Once Christ is enthroned in our hearts as Lord, He also becomes the Director of all the affairs of our life.

The supper was now brought in. First came the bitter herbs, to be dipped in salt water or vinegar and eaten. This would remind them of the bitter bondage of Egypt from which, as a nation, they had been delivered. God would ever have His people to remember the past, and recall the time when they were without God and without hope in the world. Then came the unleavened bread, which was broken and passed to each of the disciples. Finally came the roast lamb in a large dish, which was now placed on the table.

5. The announcement of the traitor in their midst (John 13:18-30)

As they were eating, there fell from the lips of the Lord the solemn announcement: "Verily, verily, I say unto you, that one of you shall betray Me!" This statement fell like a bombshell in their midst. There was a horrified hush, and we are told "they were exceeding sorrowful." After the first shock had passed away, they began to inquire of Him: "Lord, is it I?" Now notice the solemn answer of Christ, which was meant only for the ears of Judas, who had already agreed to betray Him for thirty pieces of silver: "The Son of Man goeth, as it is written of Him, but woe unto that man by whom the Son of Man is betrayed! It were good for that man if he had never been born!" (Matt. 26:24). At this, Judas had the temerity to inquire, probably in a whisper, so that none of those present might hear: "Master, is it I?" Mark the awful answer: "Thou hast said," or, "You have said it."

Our Lord here made three attempts to turn Judas from his fell purpose. First, He washed his feet. Second, He gave him the sop, as the guest of honor. Third, He sought to shock him into the realization that his perfidy was well known to Him. But all this failed to turn him from his foul design. Peter now beckoned to John, who was reclining next to the Lord, and requested him to ask the Lord who the betrayer was. On John asking the Lord, probably again in a whisper, the Lord replied: "He it is to whom I shall give the sop, when I have dipped it." This sop was the tidbit of the feast, and was usually given to the guest of honor. Then the Lord dipped the sop, and gave it to the traitor. Now mark the words: "After the sop, Satan entered into Judas. Then Christ said to him: "What thou doest, do quickly." At this, Judas went out from the feast, and John adds significantly "And it was night."

Into the black night went the black hearted traitor on his awful errand, and shortly afterwards went out into the blackness of darkness forever, to weep and wail and gnash his teeth. Probably Judas thought that the Lord, in some miraculous way, would escape from the design of His enemies, as He had done on previous occasions. Thus Judas would be richer by the thirty pieces of silver. It was when it dawned on him that he had delivered his Master to death that, filled with remorse, he cast down his ill gotten gains in the temple and rushed to a suicide's death with the bitter words upon his lips: "I have sinned, in that I have betrayed the innocent blood!"

Chapter Four

The Institution of the Lord's Supper:
Institution

The question as to whether Judas was present, or not, at the institution of the Lord's supper, has long been a matter of difference of opinion on the part of very sound and able teachers of the Word. Personally, we incline to the view that Judas was not present at the Lord's supper, and for the following reasons. The sop which the Lord gave to Judas was part of the Passover supper. On receiving this sop, we are told: "Judas immediately went out." Thus Judas *left* before the Passover meal was concluded, for the giving of the sop did not terminate the feast.

Matthew tells us that "while they were eating," Jesus took bread and instituted the Lord's supper (Matt. 26:26). This indicates that after the interruption, caused by the departure of Judas, the Passover meal was resumed. In Mark's account the same thought is expressed. We do know that it was *after* the Passover meal that the Lord's supper was instituted. If we only had Luke's account, we might conclude that Judas was present at the Lord's supper, but Luke does not always describe events in their chronological order. See, for example, Luke 3:19-22, 22:22-23. While John does not tell us of the institution of the Lord's supper, he does describe the Passover supper, and indicates at what juncture Judas left to perpetrate his foul deed and this, as we have seen, was immediately after he had received the sop.

F. W. Grant, in his *Numerical Bible*, makes this useful comment on the question. Referring to Matthew 26:26, he says: "This separation of Judas from the rest takes place before the institution of the memorial feast, which follows here: for John tells us that Judas, 'having received the sop went immediately out.' Luke inverts the order of this, and the last section; but Luke's order is often different from that of time. The point, however, is not of doctrinal importance, for few would advocate a known traitor being admitted to the table of the Lord; and if it were permitted, no discipline could be maintained at all. If Judas were present, he was yet unknown, as such, to the disciples . . . The question is therefore, as already said, of no practical importance. The principles involved are settled conclusively elsewhere."

Let us now turn our attention to the Lord's supper. We shall think of four things in connection with it. First, the setting of it. Second, the symbols He used. Third, the thanks He gave. Fourth, the request He made.

1. The setting of it

It was after the Pascal feast. Thus, while it is associated with the Passover, yet it is entirely distinct from it. It might be well to notice the contrast between the Passover and the Lord's supper.

(a) Last Passover recognized by God

This Passover was the last ever to be recognized by God, and it signified the end of the dispensation of the Law. The Lord's supper was the *first* celebration of this new ordinance, and it marked the inauguration of the dispensation of grace.

(b) Passover the memorial of a great event

This Passover was the memorial of a great event in the history of Israel, their redemption from the bondage of Egypt. The Lord's supper is the memorial of the greatest event in the history of the universe, the sacrifice of the Son of God to redeem a lost humanity.

(c) Passover designed only for Israel

This Passover was a feast especially designed for the nation of Israel. The Lord's supper is a feast especially designed for Christians only, who have been saved by His grace out of every tribe, kindred, tongue and nation.

(d) Passover necessitated slaying of animal

This Passover necessitated the slaying and eating of an animal sacrifice, a lamb without spot or blemish. The Lord's supper is a memorial of the sinless, holy, spotless Lamb of God who, in infinite grace, bore our sins and died in our stead.

(e) Passover looked forward to coming Redeemer

This Passover looked forward to a coming Redeemer who should fulfil the type of the pascal lamb. The Lord's supper looks backward to the One who accomplished, once and for ever, our eternal redemption, and yet looks onward to the time when, at His second coming, He will glorify all His people.

(f) Passover was one of many feasts

This Passover was but one of many feasts which God had given to His people Israel to observe each year, and each of which required the shedding of blood. The Lord's supper is the one ordinance by which His people may remember Him, and which was made possible by the shedding of His most precious blood. This sacrifice will never be repeated.

(g) Passover reminded Israel of atonement

This Passover reminded Israel of their sins, which required the life of a substitutionary sacrifice as an atonement. The Lord's supper provides an opportunity for Christians not only to remember the Lord Jesus, but also to be reminded that all their sins have been forgiven and forgotten because of the sacrifice of the Son of God by whom they have been reconciled to God (Rom. 5:11 margin).

2. The symbols He used

They were beautifully simple, yet tremendously profound. The bread was the picture of His body, soon to be crucified, in which He was to bear away their sins. The cup was the emblem of His blood, soon to be shed for their redemption. Both elements were available from the Passover supper, and the Lord, from these two elements, presented the great truth of His substitutionary sacrifice on their behalf. Inasmuch as we shall examine the symbolism of the bread and the cup later on, we shall confine ourselves to this brief statement at this time.

3. The thanks that He gave

Matthew, Mark and Luke refer to this, as also does Paul. The word, "giving of thanks" is "eucharisteo," from which the word, "Eucharist" is derived. We are told in Matthew 26:26 that: "Jesus took bread and blessed it." In Luke 22:19 we read: "And He took bread and gave thanks." Thus to "bless," simply means to give thanks. Ritualists make much of the word, "bless," as though this was the sole prerogative of the "officiating priest." By this act he is supposed to "consecrate the elements," and thus make possible the observance of the Lord's supper on the part of the "laity." This, of course, is wholly unwarranted from scripture, which knows nothing of an officiating priest, or any distinction between "clergy" and "laity."

The Lord Jesus, with the full knowledge of all that lay before Him in the immediate future, gave thanks. Knowing the dreadful reality of what was symbolized in the bread and the cup, He gave thanks. In the light of all that was involved in Gethsemane, Gabbatha and Golgotha, He gave thanks! This would be incredible, but for the fact that it is plainly stated in each of the accounts of the intitution of the supper. Christ has left us in no doubt as to why He came into the world: "The Son of Man came not to be ministered unto, but to minister, and to give His life a ransom for many" (Mark 10:45). Thus the cross was ever before Him every step of His earthly ministry.

We are told in Hebrews 12:2 that it was "for the joy that was set before Him" that He "endured the cross and despised the shame." This joy was the perfect fulfilling of His Father's will. He could say: "Lo I come, in the volume of the book it is written of Me, I delight to do Thy will, O My God; yea, Thy law is within My heart" (Ps. 40:8). He allowed no one to hinder Him from the complete accomplishment of His Father's will. We are told that when the time was come that He should be received up: "He stedfastly set His face to go up to Jerusalem" (Luke 9:51).

It was a lonely path He trod,
From every human soul apart;
Known only to Himself and God,
Was all the grief that filled His heart,
Yet from the track He turned not back,
Til where I lay in sin and shame,
He found me—blessed be His name!
(C. A. Tydeman)

Thus, under the frightful shadow of the blood-like sweat of Gethsemane, the cruel shame of Gabbatha, and the infinite suffering of Golgotha, our blessed Lord gave thanks for that which set forth the sacrifice of Himself! Hallelujah, what a Savior!

He also knew that, in a coming day, He would "see of the travail of His soul and be satisfied" (Isa. 53:11). He envisaged that vast multitude, which no man can number, of the redeemed of all ages who should surround His throne, and sing with adoring hearts: "Worthy is the Lamb that was slain to receive power, and riches, and wisdom, and strength, and honor, and glory and blessing!" (Rev. 5:12). In the light of all this, the blessed Son of God, in the infinitude of His grace, gave thanks. Well may we also as we give thanks for the bread and the cup, do so with adoration in our hearts for Him!

G. V. Fraser's hymn is most appropriate in this connection:

> On that same night, Lord Jesus,
> When all around Thee joined
> To cast its darkest shadow
> Across Thy holy mind,
> We hear Thy voice, blest Savior,
> "This do' remember Me:"
> With joyful hearts responding,
> We do remember Thee.
>
> The depth of all Thy suff'ring
> No heart could e'er conceive;
> The cup of wrath o'er flowing
> For us Thou didst receive;
> And oh! of God forsaken,
> On the accursed tree.
> With grateful hearts, Lord Jesus,
> We would remember Thee.
>
> We think of all the darkness
> Which round Thy spirit pressed
> Of all those waves and billows
> Which rolled across Thy breast.
> Oh, there Thy grace unbounded
> And perfect love we see;
> With joy and sorrow mingling,
> We would remember Thee.

We know Thee now as risen,
  The first-born from the dead;
We see Thee now ascended,
  The Church's glorious Head
In Thee by grace accepted,
  The heart and mind set free,
To think of all Thy sorrow,
  And thus remember Thee.

Till Thou shalt come in glory,
  And call us hence away,
To rest in all the brightness
  Of that unclouded day,
We show Thy death, Lord Jesus,
  And here would seek to be
More to Thy death conformed,
  Whilst we remember Thee.

4. The request that He made

The words are simple and admit of no other interpretation: "This do in (or, for) a remembrance of Me." The Lord's supper was therefore only intended, by the Lord Jesus, to be a memorial of Himself. It was given in order to provide an opportunity for His disciples to call Him to remembrance. There is therefore no virtue or value in the bread and the cup, save as they speak to each partaker of the Lord Jesus and the infinite cost of His redemptive work.

Christendom, by its many additions and innovations, has practically buried this simple fact beneath a rubbish heap of sacerdotalism. It has perverted what Christ intended to be a simple memorial of Himself into what is now called the sacrifice of the Mass.

Our Lord's words: "This do," should come home to each heart with peculiar force. It is said that "a king's request is his command." Here, then, is the request of the King of kings. There is only one thing for the believer to do, and that is to obey. It is one thing to sing: "Lord Jesus, I love Thee, I know Thou art mine," and another to obey Him, and do what He asks us to do, particularly in the light of the circumstances in which He made the request.

On one occasion the Lord rebuked His hearers by saying: "Why call ye Me 'Lord, Lord,' and do not the things which I say?" (Luke 6:46). It is to be feared that this request has had little effect upon some who claim to belong to Him. Perhaps through a failure to read the Word of God, and thus learn the Lord's mind for them, or through want of thought or heart, His request has gone unheeded. Sometimes the least thing is allowed to hinder believers from taking their place at the remembrance feast, and thus fulfilling His desire. James C. Deck's lovely hymn should speak to all our hearts:

> This do, remember Me—
> O blessed, living Lord,
> What depths of grace we now can trace
> In that most precious word!
>
> This do, remember Me—
> Oh, deep desire of love,
> As 'round Thy soul those waves did roll,
> God's judgment from above.
>
> This do, remember Me—
> Oh, what a savour sweet
> For God above! for man, what love,
> In all Thy work complete!
>
> Now gathered round Thyself,
> With heart and conscience free,
> O Lord, once dead, our living Head,
> We do remember Thee!

Chapter Five

The Symbolism of the Lord's Supper

Let us now spend some time in a consideration of the spiritual significance of the two elements which Christ used to symbolize His body and blood: the bread and the cup. The infinite wisdom of the Lord Jesus is seen in His selection of these two emblems. In so doing He balanced beautiful simplicity with deep spiritual profundity. What could be more simple than breaking a morsel of bread from a loaf, or taking a sip of the fruit of the vine? Yet what could be more deeply significant than what these two things combine to show forth! We must ever keep in mind that these two elements were divinely chosen. Therefore they demand our closest attention.

It is interesting to note that there was a practice among the Jews of gathering together in the home of a deceased friend, to eat bread and drink wine in his memory. (See Ezek. 24:17; Jer. 16:7; Hos. 9:4.)

The Bread

We shall think first of the bread. Upon a table is a loaf of bread and a cup containing the fruit of the vine. Around it, or before it, is a group of Christians who have gathered together in the name of the Lord Jesus, and at His invitation, to remember Him and to show forth His death till He come. What spiritual significance is conveyed to those believers as they look upon that loaf of bread?

1. The effect of a corn of wheat planted

They see the effect of a corn of wheat which was planted in the soil and died. Before that loaf could be made from the flour, many corns of wheat had to be buried in the earth and die. From those seeds, in due time, there emerged "first the blade, then the ear, after that the full corn in the ear" (Mark 4:28). Thus the bread is the result of the death of the corn of wheat. Surely this brings to mind the words of the Savior when He said: "Verily, verily, I say unto you, except a corn of wheat fall into the ground and die, it abideth alone: but if it die, it bringeth forth much fruit" (John 12:24).

Our Lord came into this world in order that He might die for our sins. It was for this very cause that He became incarnate. We are told: "He took not on Him the nature of angels, but He took on Him the seed of Abraham." As God, He could not die, but, as Man, He could and, in His wondrous grace did die "for our sins according to the Scriptures" (Heb. 2:16; 1 Cor. 15:3-4). We are also informed He was: "made a little lower than the angels for the suffering of death." We also read: "Forasmuch as the children were partakers of flesh and blood, He also Himself likewise took part of the same; that through death, He might destroy him that had the power of death, that is the Devil" (Heb. 2:9-14).

The death of our Lord was both *voluntary* and *vicarious*. He declared: "Therefore doth My Father love Me, because I lay down My life that I might take it again. No man taketh My life from Me, but I lay it down of Myself. I have power (authority) to lay it down, and I have power to take it again. This commandment have I received of My Father" (John 10:17-18). Christ was absolutely sinless, pure and holy. We are told He had no sin, knew no sin and did no sin (1 John 3:5; 2 Cor. 5:21; 1 Peter 2:22). Death, therefore, had no claim upon Him, for death is the result of sin. His death therefore was purely *voluntary*. He also declared: "I am the good Shepherd, the good Shepherd giveth His life for the sheep" (John 10:11). By this He indicated that His death was *vicarious*, or on behalf of others. His very name was given Him because of the work He was to accomplish. "Thou shalt call His name Jesus, for He shall save His people from their sins" (Matt. 1:21).

Any boy or girl, if given enough time, can count the number of acorns on an oak tree, but no man can possibly compute how many oak trees there are in an acorn, providing that acorn is placed in the ground and dies. In so doing, it will reproduce itself in an oak tree. Now plant the acorns from that tree and, in turn, all the acorns produced by those trees and soon the whole world will be carpeted with oak trees. Think of the millions of people who, through faith in the substitutionary sacrifice of Christ and acceptance of Him as their personal Savior, have become the possessors of eternal life! Each one will gladly trace it all to the One who, as the Corn of wheat, died for his sins and rose again for his justification (Rom. 4:25).

2. The result of wheat being ground

These believers also realize that the loaf of bread is the result of many kernels of wheat being ground between the upper and nether millstone, and thus reduced to flour. That scripture will come to mind, where we read: "Bread corn is bruised," and they will link with this the well known words of Isaiah: "He was wounded for our transgressions, He was bruised for our iniquities: the chastisement of our peace was upon Him, and with His stripes we are healed" (Isa. 28:28, 53:5).

This will speak to their hearts particularly of the *physical* sufferings of Christ at the hands of the very creatures in whom He had placed the breath of life. They will call to mind the blood-like sweat of Gethsemane, where Christ said: "My soul is exceeding sorrowful, even unto death," and where, "being in an agony, He prayed more earnestly, and His sweat was, as it were, great drops of blood falling to the ground" (Matt. 26:38; Luke 22:44). They will follow Him in thought, from the garden to Gabbatha, where He was given a mock trial before Pilate who, to his everlasting shame, condemned to death One whom he knew to be innocent. Mocked, beaten, spat upon and crowned with thorns, He was led as a lamb to the slaughter. "He gave His back to the smiter, and His cheek to them that plucked off the hair" (Isa. 50:6).

They will then envision Him as He came to Golgotha, the place of the skull. Bearing His own cross, He mounted the slopes of the hill, stretched out His hands upon the cross, and allowed Himself to be nailed to the tree. Who can estimate the awful suffering He endured during those hours upon the cross? Who can fathom the meaning of those words: "Christ also hath suffered for sins, the Just for the unjust, that He might bring us to God" (1 Peter 3:18)? Truly, "Bread corn is bruised," and Christ went through the millstones of God's judgment for us—blessed be His name!

No Christian, as he muses upon these things can remain unmoved. With the poet he reverently sings:

> Crowned with thorns upon the tree,
>   Silent in Thine agony;
> Dying crushed beneath the load
>   Of the wrath and curse of God.
>
> On Thy pale and suffering brow,
>   Mystery of love and woe;
> On Thy grief and sore amaze,
>   Savior, I would fix my gaze.

Sin atoning Sacrifice,
  Thou art precious in mine eyes;
Thou alone my rest shalt be,
  Now and through eternity.
(Gratton Gumness)

3. The result of being baked in an oven

They also see, in the loaf, a picture of the unseen spiritual sufferings of their Savior. Just as the dough must be placed in the oven and, unseen to human eyes, is subjected to the fierce heat of the fire, ere it can become a loaf of bread, so Christ, during those three hours of darkness on the cross was shut up to God, who "made to meet upon Him the iniquity of us all" (Isa. 53:6). In that lone, dark and mysterious hour, our Lord suffered at the hands of God, who dealt with Him on account of our sin. Inasmuch as He had assumed the liability of all our guilt, He must therefore endure, at the hands of a holy God, all the judgment that those sins deserved.

The whole question of sin was brought into account and dealt with by a holy and righteous God, "who can by no means clear the guilty" (Ex. 34:7). Therefore, upon the head of our divine Substitute, as He hung upon the cross, there was poured out the full judgment that divine justice demanded. No human mind can possibly fathom the infinite sufferings through which our blessed Lord passed as He hung upon that tree, surrounded by that awful darkness, despised and rejected of men, and then forsaken of His God.

It is in the Psalms that the unseen, *spiritual* sufferings of Christ are described. We hear Him saying: "Deep calleth unto deep at the noise of Thy waterspouts: all Thy waves and billows have gone over Me." Again He cries: "I sink in deep mire where there is no standing. I am come into deep waters where the floods overflow Me." Once more we hear His orphaned cry: "My God, My God, why hast Thou forsaken Me? Why art Thou so far from helping Me, and from the words of My roaring? O My God, I cry in the daytime, but Thou hearest not, and in the night season, and am not silent. But Thou art holy, O Thou that inhabitest the praises of Israel" (Ps. 42:7, 69:2, 22:1-3). Thus, in the horror of that darkness, unseen by man, all the righteous judgment of God against sin fell, in all its infinite severity, on His sinless, unprotected head until He had satisfied, to the full, all the demands of God against sin and the sinner. Then, and only then, did He cry with a loud triumphant voice: "It is finished!" and bowed His head and dismissed His spirit. Thus the loaf of bread speaks eloquently, to the believer, of both the *physical* and the *spiritual* sufferings of his Lord.

F. C. Jennings has beautifully expressed it in the following lines:

> Agony of agonies!
> This the pain of Calvary:
> Bow, my soul, in solemn awe,
> From thy foot thy sandal draw:
> This is truly holy ground,
> Here is mystery profound.
> Few thy words—but let thy thought
> Be with deep emotion fraught:
> Tremble, whilst Truth speaks to Guilt,
> Telling why that blood was spilt;
> Weep, e'en whilst sweet Mercy's voice
> Bids thy broken heart rejoice;
> Praise while Love and Truth unite,
> Flooding heart with heavenly light
> Trembling, weeping, praising, learn
> (Let it in thy spirit burn)
> Thy sins—thyself—hast caused that cry—
> 'Eli lama sabachthani!'

The Cup

By the side of the loaf there is a cup containing the fruit of the vine. It also is full of spiritual significance, for it is the symbol of that by which the believer has been redeemed. Let us listen to the Savior's own words concerning the cup: "This cup is the new testament in My blood which is shed for you" (Luke 22:20). Thus the cup, (by which, of course, the contents are meant) was the divinely ordained symbol of the precious blood of Christ, by which our eternal salvation has been secured.

Wine, as we know, is obtained by pressing the grape. Hence, in the olden days, the wine press was used, in which the grapes were usually trodden down by the feet of men. (See Neh. 13:5; Job 24:11.) In this way the juice was extracted then drawn off and placed either in skins or in earthern vessels, until the desired process of fermentation was completed. Wine was often referred to as "the blood of the grape" (Gen. 49:11; Deut. 32:14).

Hence our Lord selected the fruit of the vine to symbolize His precious blood, or His outpoured life on our behalf.

One has only to read the Old Testament, and particularly the book of Leviticus, to be impressed with the fact that the shedding of the blood of animal sacrifices was an integral part of the ritual connected with approaching God. This is seen in both the tabernacle and later, in the temple. The New Testament summarizes this fact in the well known words of Hebrews 9:22: "And almost all things are by the law purged with blood; and without the shedding of blood is no remission." There can be no approach to God, no forgiveness from God, and no acceptance with God apart from a substitutionary sacrifice. God views the sacrifice as taking the place of the sinner, bearing the sins of the sinner and dying in the stead of the sinner. Thus the sinner is accepted by God in his offering.

The key phrase of Leviticus, which sums up the whole purpose of the offerings, is found in Leviticus 1:4. It is stated here: "And he (the sinner) shall put his hand upon the head of the burnt offering, and it (the offering) shall be accepted for him." By the placing of his hands upon the head of his offering, the sinner thus identified himself with his sacrifice. This sacrifice now became his substitute in the sight of God, bore his sins and died in his stead, that he might be accepted before God.

All these sacrifices of the Old Testament looked forward to the advent of Christ, who would completely fulfil them by the sacrifice of Himself. Because of His finished work, the Lord Jesus has made possible the acceptance of every sinner who will trust solely in His redeeming work and receive Him as his own personal Savior. Thus, as believers look upon the cup, several things will suggest themselves to their minds. Let us think of four of these things concerning the blood.

1. The significance of the blood

Perhaps the greatest statement in regard to this is found in Leviticus 17:11 where we read: "For the life of the flesh is in the blood: and I have given it to you upon the altar to make an atonement for your souls: for it is the blood that maketh an atonement for the soul." Here the great principle is stated that the blood represents the life. Therefore when the Lord Jesus said of the contents of the cup: "This is the new testament in My blood," the disciples realized that the Lord was saying He was about to give His life for them.

2. The necessity for the blood

We have already seen that "without the shedding of blood there is no remission." When Christ came into the world He affirmed: "Think not that I am come to destroy the law or the prophets: I am not come to destroy but to fulfil [fill full]" (Matt. 5:17). All the sacrifices of the Old Testament were but "shadows," or pictures of Him who was to come (Heb. 8:5, 10:1). Christ came to be the substance, the reality, and the antitype of all the many offerings that combined to set Him forth. All that the law demanded for the forgiveness of the sinner, Christ has paid to the uttermost. One of the great statements that summarizes this fact is found in Heb. 9:14: "For if the blood of bulls and of goats, and the ashes of an heifer sprinkling the unclean, sanctifieth to the purifying of the flesh: how much more shall the blood of Christ, who—through the eternal Spirit offered Himself without spot to God, purge your conscience from dead works to serve the living God?"

3. The shedding of the blood

When that great moment came, predestinated from a past eternity, the Son of God, in the calm dignity of His eternal Godhead, mounted the slopes of Golgotha's hill, stretched Himself out upon the cross, and allowed wicked men to nail Him there. He knew that only by the shedding of His blood could our salvation be secured. By His death, all the claims of the law have been met, together with all the demands of divine justice. All the work needed for the salvation of every sinner who will trust Him has been accomplished to God's complete satisfaction. The cross is the focal center of the universe, and the supreme fact of all time. The blood, which a holy God demanded for our redemption, has been shed by the Son of God, and God has accepted the payment and issued His receipt, the resurrection.

> Christ, the Lord, is risen!
> Victory is won:
> All the work that saves the
> Sinner has been done!
> Now, through faith in Him, God
> Offers full and free:
> Pardon, peace and joy and
> Glorious liberty!

4. The efficacy of the precious blood of Christ

One statement of Scripture comes to mind: "The blood of Jesus Christ, His Son, cleanseth us from all sin" (1 John 1:7). By this is meant that the sacrifice of Christ is the perpetual and all sufficient answer to all our sin. The sacrifices of the law could only *atone* for sin. The word, "atone," means to cover. The sacrifices of the Old Testament could not *put away* sins, they could only *cover* them up. We are definitely told this in so many words: "It is not possible that the blood of bulls and goats should take away sins" (Heb. 10:4). God only accepted these offerings in view of what His beloved Son should accomplish when He came into the world to "put away sin by the sacrifice of Himself" (Heb. 9:26).

The poet has again expressed it beautifully:

Not all the blood of beasts,
On Jewish altars slain,
Could give the guilty conscience peace,
Or wash away its stain.

But Christ, the heavenly Lamb,
Took all our sins away,
A sacrifice of nobler name
And richer blood than they.

We now look back to see
The burden Thou didst bear,
When hanging on the accursed tree,
For all our guilt was there.

Believing, we rejoice
To see the curse remove;
We bless the Lamb with cheerful voice,
And sing redeeming love.

(Isaac Watts)

Thus, as the believer views the cup and realizes, in a measure, all that it implies, his heart will be moved to praise and worship the One who has bought him with His precious blood. Each time he comes to the Lord's supper he will be reminded that he has "not been redeemed with corruptible things . . . but with the precious blood of Christ, as of a Lamb without blemish and without spot" (1 Peter 1:18). As he thus lifts up his heart in adoration to Christ, he is but one of very many thousands of other Christians who are doing the same thing. In a coming day, a vast throng shall surround the Lamb upon the throne, and shall sing, with glorious harmony and exquisite cadence: "Thou art worthy . . . for Thou wast slain, and hast redeemed us to God, by Thy blood, out of every kindred, and tongue, and people and nation; and hast made us unto our God kings and priests: and we shall reign on the earth" (Rev. 5:9-10).

May it be ours to have an ever increasing appreciation of the wonderful symbolism of the bread and the cup. Let us never forget, however, that they were only appointed by the Lord to *focus* our attention upon Himself. The symbols are temporary, for they are only "till He come." The time is coming when we shall no longer require the emblems to remind us of Him, for we shall see Him as He is and be forever with and like Him!

Chapter Six

The Purpose of the Lord's Supper:
Remembrance of His Person

Scripture leaves us in no doubt as to the purpose of the Lord's supper. The One who instituted it stated this very definitely: "This do for a remembrance of Me" (Luke 22:19). It is when we turn to the special revelation given by the Lord to Paul that we learn of three more purposes Christ had in mind, namely: the discernment of His body, the proclamation of His death and the anticipation of His return. All four of these purposes are found in 1 Corinthians 11:20-34.

In this epistle, Paul, by divine inspiration, rebukes the believers at Corinth for the disorders which prevailed at what they mistakenly called "the Lord's supper." They had turned this ordinance into a common meal, in which each one gratified his own appetite for food and drink. In fact, some of them had become so intemperate that they were actually intoxicated! Not only so, but they were guilty of making class distinctions, for some had plenty of food while others went hungry.

This is why he said, when referring to this common meal: "When ye come together therefore in one place, this is not to eat the Lord's supper. For in eating every one taketh before another his own supper: and one is hungry and another is drunken" (vs. 20-21). This failure to distinguish between their own supper and the Lord's supper had resulted in confusion in the assembly, and Paul points out that God, most emphatically, is "not the Author of confusion, but of peace, as in all churches of the saints" (1 Cor. 14:33).

As a result of their disorderly conduct, and failure to appreciate what was meant by the Lord's supper, many of them were weak and sickly, and some had actually been taken away by the hand of death. Paul now proceeded to tell them just exactly what the Lord's supper was, and what the Lord's purpose was in instituting it, so that they would be spiritually intelligent in their observance of it in the future.

It is interesting to notice the additional details which the Lord gave to Paul concerning this ordinance. This serves to illustrate the fact that all the great doctrines of the Christian faith, which are expounded in the epistles, are found, in germ, in the gospels. Christ had to say to His disciples: "I have yet many things to say unto you, but ye cannot bear them now. Howbeit when He, the Spirit of truth is come, He will guide you into all truth" (John 16:12-13). Paul had not been present on that fateful night when the Lord's supper had been instituted, hence the Lord Himself had directly revealed to him both the circumstances, order, significance and purpose of it.

There are five such additional details found in 1 Corinthians 11 which are not revealed in the Gospels. They are as follows:

First, the Lord's supper was a proclamation of His death (v. 26).

Second, there is the necessity for self examination and self judgment before partaking of the elements (vs. 28, 31).

Third, there must be a spiritual discernment of the Lord's body in the partaking of it (v. 29).

Fourth, careless participation may result in the chastening hand of the Lord upon them (v. 30).

Fifth, the Lord's supper is only to be observed until the coming of the Lord (v. 26).

How thankful we should be for this further revelation concerning this ordinance. Paul speaks of four such special revelations which he received directly from the Lord Himself, namely:

First, the proclamation and content of the gospel (1 Cor. 15:1-3).

Second, the truth of the Church, its formation, constitution, order, gifts and its consummation at His coming (Eph. 3:1-6).

Third, the commemoration of the Lord's supper (1 Cor. 11).

Fourth, the translation of the Church at the second coming of the Lord Jesus (1 Thess. 4:13-18; 1 Cor. 15:51-58).

Now let us consider the purpose of the Lord's supper which, as we have indicated, is fourfold: (1) the remembrance of His person (2) the discerning of His body (3) the proclamation of His death (4) the anticipation of His return.

The Remembrance of His Person

This is seen in the twice repeated words: "This do in [for a] remembrance of Me." From this, we are impressed with the heart's desire of our blessed Lord to be remembered by His redeemed people. As the Lord looked down the corridor of the ages yet unborn, He saw how much we would need this constant remembrance of Himself in the taking of the bread and the drinking of the cup. Well He knew how forgetful and fickle His people would be. As the Creator of man, He knew his complex personality, and how short a memory he would have of certain things.

In view of this, He instituted this simple ordinance, and explained its purpose: "This do for a remembrance of Me." From that time on, companies of believers, large and small, have gathered together in His name alone and, in Scriptural simplicity, have sought to carry out the request of the One, "whom, having not seen they love."

Let us suppose that a person receives two letters by the same mail. One letter contains an invitation to attend a lecture by a world famous and eloquent speaker on the subject of: "His majesty the king, as I know him." The other letter is an invitation from the king himself, inviting him to dinner at the royal palace. Both invitations are scheduled for the same evening.

Now which of these two invitations is this person most likely to accept? The one to hear a lecture about the king by one who knows him well; or the one to meet the king himself and dine with him? The answer will surely be obvious to all.

This explains the difference between going to hear an address by a well known and gifted preacher of the word of God, and going to meet the Lord Himself at the supper which He instituted, and to which He invites all His blood-bought people. It is to be feared that many believers have never learned to distinguish between going to hear a sermon about the Lord Jesus, and the more excellent thing of gathering in the presence of the Lord Himself, to remember Him, and pour out their hearts in adoring wonder and worship as they sense the beauty, excellency and glory of the One who is "the chiefest of ten thousand," and "the altogether lovely" (Song 5:10, 16).

Thus, the principal purpose that brings His people to this supper is not to preach the gospel to the unsaved, or to hear a learned exposition of

Scripture from some gifted teacher, or to listen to the beautiful voices of a well trained choir, or to have the great need of the foreign mission field brought before them, or even to engage in the holy act of intercession in prayer on behalf of others. All these things are very well in their place, but this is not the purpose of this meeting. The sole purpose of the Lord's supper is to provide an opportunity for the Lord's people to concentrate their mind's attention and their heart's affection on the Person of the Lord Jesus Christ, to the exclusion of all else.

Since the remembrance of the Lord Jesus is the supreme object of this ordinance, it follows that anything which is introduced that would distract the mind from this purpose must be rigidly excluded. Many Christians bemoan the fact that their minds often wander during this remembrance meeting so that, instead of fulfilling the request of their Lord in remembering Him, they have allowed their thoughts to wander into the forbidden fields of fancy. Thus the Lord has been robbed of His portion and they, in turn, have missed the blessedness which comes from occupation with Him.

This concentration of one's mind on a single subject for any length of time is not easy, but it can be accomplished by constant practice. It calls for a deliberate exercise of the will, by which any wandering thoughts are arrested and brought back to the purpose of the gathering, and the subject that should occupy the mind. Sometimes young believers ask: "What should be my thoughts as I sit at the Lord's supper, and how can I best control these thoughts to the glory of the Lord Jesus during the entire period of the meeting?"

We will suggest seven things that may well occupy the mind of each believer as, in obedience to his Lord, he gathers with his fellow believers at the Lord's supper. As he views the bread and the cup, what shall he remember?

1. Remember His name

In Ps. 20:7 we read: "Some trust in chariots and some in horses; but we will remember the name of the Lord, our God." Concentration on the names of the Lord is bound to produce worship. In Scripture, God's names combine to reveal His character. Note what He declares: "I am Jehovah, that is My name, and My glory will I not give to another!" (Isa. 42:8). Well sang the poet:

How sweet the name of Jesus sounds
  In a believer's ear.

Think of Him as "Jesus," the name given Him at His birth. It means "Jehovah-Savior." "Thou shalt call His name Jesus, for He shall save His people from their sins" (Matt. 1:21). What thoughts this should stir in the Christian's breast! Think of Him as "the Christ," or the anointed One of God, who so perfectly translated the will of His Father in terms of a life of perfect obedience to His will, even unto death (Acts 2:36). Think of Him as "Lord," the One whom God hath highly exalted, and given "a name that is above every name." Think of Him as the One who is called: "Wonderful, Counsellor, the mighty God, the Father of eternity and the Prince of peace" (Isa. 9:6). Think of Him as the "Word," the Logos (John 1:1-5). Language has aptly been described as "the incarnation of thought." Just as our thoughts are clothed by and expressed to others by means of words, so Christ, as the living Word, has revealed God, in all the glory of His being, and the full display of all His divine attributes.

Thou art the everlasting Word,
  The Father's only Son;
God manifestly seen and heard,
  And heaven's beloved One!

(J. Condor)

"His name is as ointment poured forth" (Song 1:3). As we concentrate on His name, and all that it unfolds to us of His infinite worth and exquisite loveliness, there will ascend from our hearts the sweet incense of worship that brings delight to His heart (John 4:23).

2. Remember His works

In 1 Chronicles 15:25-16:3, there is a description of David's removal of the ark of the Lord from the house of Obed Edom to a tent he had specially prepared for it. As the ark, the symbol of the presence of the Lord with His people, was set up in the midst of the tent, the people of God lifted their voices in praise. On that day David delivered a psalm into the hands of Asaph to commemorate the glad occasion. In this song occur the words: "Remember His marvelous works that He hath done!" (1 Chron. 16:12). Well might the believer, as he gathers with his fellow saints, and with the Lord Himself in the midst, heed these words of "the sweet singer of Israel" (2 Sam. 23:2).

Think of His marvelous works in creation, for all things were created by the Lord Jesus (Col 1:16). The vast universe, of which this earth of ours is but a microscopic speck, came into being at His command: "He spake and it was done; He commanded and it stood fast" (Ps. 33:9). As the great "Master Workman" he created man in His own image, breathed into his nostrils the breath of life, and thus caused him to become a living soul (Gen. 2:7). But all these marvelous works fade into utter insignificance in comparison to the mighty work of redemption. which He accomplished at the infinite cost of the sacrifice of Himself.

When to the cross I turn mine eyes,
And rest on Calvary;
O Lamb of God, my Sacrifice,
I must remember Thee.
(J. Montgomery)

It was this work that He came to do, lived to accomplish and died to consummate (Luke 2:49; John 4:34; 19:30). The believer, as he remembers this marvelous work, can now thankfully exclaim: "For Thou, Lord, has made me glad through Thy work: I will triumph in the work of Thy hands!" (Ps. 92:4).

3. Remember His love

"We will be glad and rejoice in Thee, we will remember Thy love more than wine" (Song 1:4). As the believer concentrates on that "love of Christ, that passeth knowledge," the breadth and length and height and depth of which is beyond all human ken, he will soon find himself beyond his depth and be lost in wonder, love and praise, and his soul flooded with precious thoughts of "love, so amazing, so divine" (Eph. 3:19).

The evident proof of His love is seen on the table in the bread and the cup: His body given and His blood shed. As the believer contemplates that love, all cold formality must surely melt, and there shall rise from his heart a good measure of appreciation of His infinite love and grace. The deeps of the love of Christ will call to the deeps of his being, and he will gladly respond: "I love Him, because He first loved me." (See 1 John 4:19.)

We could remember many things about His love. The Scripture assures us it is immeasureable, incomprehensible, eternal, inseparable, irrefutable, unchangeable, and unquenchable. (See Eph. 3:18-19; Jer. 31:3; Rom. 8:35-39;

1 John 4:9; John 13:1; Song 8:7.) Yes, there will be plenty to occupy our thoughts as we dwell upon His love!

4. Remember His affliction

Christ, speaking prophetically through Jeremiah, says, "Remember My affliction and My misery, the wormwood and the gall" (Lam. 3:19, marg.). Here the believer stands on holy ground, and the hush of eternity falls upon his spirit as he contemplates the awful sufferings of the Son of God, by which his salvation was accomplished.

The Savior draws near and whispers, as it were: "Remember that I became the Man of sorrows and acquainted with grief. Remember that I suffered the contradiction of sinners against Myself, and endured the cross and despised the shame. Remember, that all the floodgates of the infinite judgment of God rolled over My spotless soul as I hung upon the cross bearing all your sins in My own body. Remember, I was forsaken of God in that lone, dark and mysterious hour, and that I drained, to its last dark and bitter drop, the cup of suffering. Remember that I did it all for you, that you might have your sins forgiven, be at peace with God, and blessed with all the spiritual blessings you now enjoy. Therefore remember My affliction and My misery, the wormwood and the gall."

In verse 20 of that same chapter is found the response of the one who has fulfilled the Lord's request. Filled with reverential awe, the believer adoringly replies: "My soul hath them still in remembrance, and is bowed within me" (Lam. 3:20).

Gethsemane, can I forget,
  And there Thy conflict see,
Thine agony and blood-like sweat,
  And not remember Thee?
(J. Montgomery)

5. Remember His exaltation

Paul could triumphantly exclaim: "Remember that Jesus Christ was raised from the dead according to my gospel!" (2 Tim. 2:8). At the Lord's supper, we not only meet to remember One who suffered, bled and died, but also One who rose, and now lives in the power of an endless life. By faith we see Him glorified at the right hand of the majesty on high, our great high Priest, who "ever liveth to make intercession for us." We apprehend the glorious truth that: "Christ, being raised from the dead dieth no more; death hath no more dominion over Him. For in that He died, He died unto sin once (for all): but in that He liveth, He liveth unto God" (Rom. 6:9-10).

The cross, and all its shame, is now for ever past:

Never more shall God, Jehovah
  Smite the Shepherd with the sword;
Never more shall cruel sinners
  Set at nought our glorious Lord!
(R. C. Chapman)

Thus we remember Him as the One whom God has exalted, "Far above all principality, and power, and might, and dominion, and every name that is named, not only in this world, but also in that which is to come: and hath put all things under His feet, and gave Him to be Head over all things to the Church, which is His body, the fulness of Him that filleth all in all" (Eph. 1:21-23). Thus we sing:

Rise my soul, behold 'tis Jesus!
  Jesus fills thy wondering eyes;
See Him there, in glory seated,
  Where thy sins no more can rise!
(J. Denham Smith)

Gazing on the Lord in glory,
  While our hearts in worship bow;
There we read the wondrous story
  Of the cross, its shame and woe.
(Miss C. Thompson)

As by faith we enter through the new and living way, into the holiest of all, we can therefore "worship the Lord in the beauty of holiness" and thus fulfil the purpose for which He saved us by His grace (Ps. 96:9).

6. Remember His mercies

Paul exhorted the saints at Ephesus to remember the kindness and the love of God which He had shown them in their salvation. Note his words: "Wherefore remember, that ye being in time past Gentiles in the flesh . . . that at that time ye were without Christ, . . . having no hope, and without

God in the world: But now, in Christ Jesus, ye who sometimes were far off, are made nigh by the blood of Christ" (Eph. 2:11-13).

It is a good thing to remember the black past of our unsaved days, and contrast it with the bright present of our blessedness in Christ, and remember that it is all due to the super-abounding and sovereign grace of God as revealed in the gift of His dear Son.

Surely no believer can remain unmoved as he recalls the happy day when he trusted Christ as his personal Savior, and was assured, by the word of God, of his acceptance in the Beloved. Yes, we do well to remember the goodness and the multitudinous mercies of the Lord, which have followed us all the days of our life! Like the psalmist, we can lift up our hearts and voices and say: "I will sing of the mercies of the Lord for ever: with my mouth will I make known thy faithfulness to all generations!" (Ps. 89:1).

There is a Persian story of one who had been raised from a lowly station in life to a high position in royal favor. In his palace one room was dedicated as a "Chamber of Memory." There he kept memorials of earlier days—the days before he was elevated to the lofty place. The floors were bare. A crook, a wallet, a water cruse, a coarse dress—things belonging to the shepherd life were there. Every day he spent one hour in this room. He lived again among the memories of his youth. These recollections not only kept him humble, but contributed to his happiness and gave him a warm heart for the common people. Such daily thoughts will prepare us for the actual remembrance supper each Lord's day.

7. Remember His words

In his farewell speech to the elders of the church at Ephesus, Paul said: "Ye ought to support the weak, and to remember the words of the Lord Jesus, how He said: 'It is more blessed to give than to receive'" (Acts 20:35). As we sit in His presence at the Lord's supper, we would do well to remember His words. This cannot be done unless we have read these words, and stored them in our memories. This involves the systematic reading, study and memorization of the holy Scriptures, which is a must for all believers. All will do well to make this a habit from the very commencement of their Christian lives.

Much poverty of soul is directly attributable to the failure of the private, regular and devotional reading of the Word. We are exhorted to "Let the word of Christ dwell in you richly in all wisdom" (Col. 3:16). As we call to mind some of the words of our Savior and meditate upon them, we shall discover, as did those disciples on the road to Emmaus, that our hearts will burn within us as He communes with us by the way (Luke 24:25-32).

As we think of His words of gracious invitation, of assuring love, of satisfying consolation and of glorious anticipation, we shall discover that the fire will burn in our souls, and our tongues shall also become as "the pen of a ready writer," and we shall speak of things touching the King (Ps. 39:3; 45:1). No wonder Jeremiah exclaimed: "Thy words were found, and I did eat them; and Thy word was unto me the joy and rejoicing of mine heart: for I "am called by Thy name, O Lord God of Hosts" (Jer. 15:16).

It is surely fitting on such occasions to sing James Montgomery's beautiful hymn:

ACCORDING TO THY GRACIOUS WORD

According to Thy gracious word,
In deep humility
This would I do, O Christ, my Lord,
I would remember Thee.

Thy body, given for my sake,
My bread from heav'n shall be:
Thy testamental cup I take,
And thus remember Thee.

Remember Thee, and all Thy pains,
And all Thy love to me;
Yea, while a breath—a pulse remains,
Would I remember Thee.

And when, O Lord, Thou com'st again,
And I Thy glory see,
Forever as the Lamb once slain,
I will remember Thee.

Chapter Seven

The Purpose of the Lord's Supper:
Illustration from Life of Joseph

A lovely illustration of the desire of our Lord Jesus to be remembered is seen in the life of Joseph, who is perhaps one of the most complete personal types of our Lord in the Old Testament scriptures. After he had interpreted for good the butler's dream he said to him: "Remember me when it shall be well with thee, and show kindness, I pray thee, unto me, and make mention of me unto Pharoah, and bring me out of this house" (Gen. 40:14). Let us note five distinct things suggested in these words.

(a) The necessary prerequisite, "When it shall be well with thee"

It is only as it is well with our souls that we can fittingly remember Him. Such a meeting as the Lord's supper, scripturally observed, has no attraction for an unsaved person. He would vote it as the driest and dreariest of meetings, and for a very good reason: it wasn't well with him! Such a person is without God, Christ, life, peace and hope. Over him hangs the dark cloud of the wrath of God, which is "revealed from heaven against all sin and unrighteousness" (Eph. 2:11-12; Rom. 1:18-19).

It is only the person who knows Christ as his Savior, God as his Father, and the Holy Spirit as his indwelling Comforter who can truthfully sing that hymn:

> My sin, O the bliss of this glorious thought,
> My sin, not in part, but the whole,
> Is nailed to that cross, and I bear it no more:
> Bless the Lord! Bless the Lord, O my soul!
> It is well, It is well with my soul!
> (H. G. Spafford)

(b) The desired remembrance, "Remember me"

Having realized the "blessedness of the man whose transgressions are forgiven," the believer is now in a position to remember the One who made his forgiveness possible by bearing those sins "in His own body on the tree" (Ps. 32:1; 1 Peter 2:24). How shall those who are saved remember their Lord? The answer is simple. Gather with a company of believers at the Lord's supper. Take of the bread and the cup, sweet memorials of His infinite love. In this simple way, which the Lord Himself ordained, each Christian can fulfil the request of his Lord and Savior.

As he thus meets with the Lord's people each Lord's day, he will be led to reverently and adoringly sing:

> Savior, we remember Thee,
>   Thy deep woe and agony;
> All Thy suffering on the tree:
>   Savior, we adore Thee!
>
> (S. T. Francis)

(c) The grateful recompense, "Show kindness . . . unto me"

Joseph here says, in effect: "Inasmuch as I have shown you a kindness, now show me a kindness." Does the Lord Jesus, now glorified in heaven, want us to show kindness to Him? Yes, indeed. We can show kindness to Him by showing kindness to all who belong to Him. The Lord laid down a principle which has never been abrogated. Mark His words: "Inasmuch as ye have done it unto one of these, the least of My brethren, ye have done it unto Me" (Matt. 25:40). This clearly teaches that any kindness shown to one who belongs to Christ, is a kindness done to the Lord Himself.

It will be recalled that He also said: "Whosoever shall give you a cup of water to drink, because ye belong to Christ, verily I say unto you, he shall not lose his reward" (Mark 9:41). Again we read: "Be not forgetful to entertain strangers, for thereby some have entertained angels unawares . . . But to do good and to communicate forget not, for with such sacrifices God is well pleased" (Heb. 12:2, 16).

Here is our warrant for *practical* Christianity. This will keep the believer busy for the rest of the week. He is exhorted to show loving kindness to all who know the Lord. He is to exhibit the grace of hospitality. He is to "do good unto all men," his unsaved neighbors, who need the help and comfort that only He can give them in their need, and "especially to them who are of the household of faith" (Gal. 6:10). In this way believers can reciprocate the kindness which the Lord has shown to them, and realize the truth of His words when He said: "It is more blessed to give than to receive" (Acts 20:35).

(d) The faithful recommendation, "Make mention of Me"

Joseph desired the recommendation of this butler who would, on his release, have the ear of the king of Egypt. Egypt, as we know, is a type of the world which "lies in the arms of the wicked" one, and lives in the darkness of sin, ignorance, superstition, unbelief and enmity to God. How are poor worldlings ever to hear the good news of the gospel unless those, who know Christ, tell them the "old, old story of Jesus and His love"?

Our Lord's commission should come as a challenge to every Christian: "Go ye into all the world and preach the gospel to every creature" (Mark 16:15). The preaching of the gospel consists of making mention of the Lord Jesus to others, for Christ is the center, theme and circumference of the gospel. This preaching does not necessarily mean the formal preaching of a sermon from a platform, but includes private and individual witness to others as the opportunity presents itself. It can be done by judicious tract distribution, by hospital and jail visitation, by the teaching of a Sunday School class, and a host of other means. The great need of the world today is the personal recommendation of Christ, both by word and by life on the part of Christians.

(e) The longed for release, "Bring me out of this house"

Joseph, at this time, was still in the place of rejection. He had been despised by his brethren, and unjustly accused by his master. In the same way our Lord, as far as this world is concerned, is still rejected and His claims disallowed. The time is coming, however, when He will come forth from the place where He now is and, like Joseph, will take His proper place as the supreme One.

We can get a glimpse of the longing of our Lord from 2 Thessalonians 3:5, where we read: "The Lord direct your hearts into the love of God, and the patience of Christ" (marg.). Thus our Lord is waiting, with patience, for that glad moment when He will return, according to His own promise. What cheer these words of His have brought to millions of believers: "Let not your heart be troubled: ye believe in God, believe also in Me. In My Father's house are many mansions, if it were not so, I would have told you. I go to prepare a place for you. And if I go and prepare a place for you, I will come again, and receive you unto Myself; that where I am, there ye may be also" (John 14:1-3).

What a day of days that shall be, when the silence of heaven shall be broken with "the voice of the archangel and the trump of God," and all the redeemed shall be taken to be with Him for ever! The last prayer of the Bible is concerned with this great event, "Even so, come, Lord Jesus" (Rev. 22:20).

Little did that butler realize that the preservation of the empire of Egypt was dependent on his mentioning of Joseph to Pharoah. It was only when he did so, after a long period of forgetfulness, that Joseph came forth from the prison to take his place among the world's immortals. May it be ours, likewise, to do all in our power to hasten the day when our Lord, who is now rejected, will come into His own and be given His rightful place of preeminence.

Let all that look for, hasten
That coming joyful day,
By earnest consecration,
To walk the narrow way,
By gathering in the lost ones,
For whom our Lord did die,
For the crowning day that's coming by and by!
(D. W. Whittle)

May the Lord be pleased to "stir up our pure hearts by way of remembrance," so that when we come together to eat the bread and drink of the cup, we shall do it in a worthy manner, and thus fulfil the desire of our blessed Lord when He said, "This do for a remembrance of Me."

Chapter Eight

The Purpose of the Lord's Supper:
Discerning the Body of Christ: Transubstantiation

The Discerning of the Body of Christ

We are told: "He that eateth and drinketh unworthily, eateth and drinketh judgment (marg.) to himself, not discerning the Lord's body" (1 Cor. 11:29). We shall spend some time in considering the meaning of these words. In what way does the believer "discern the Lord's body" as he takes the Lord's supper? What did our Lord intend to convey to His disciples by the words: "This is My body . . . This is My blood"? Did He mean that His words should be taken *literally*, or were they to understand that He spoke to them in *figurative* language? Do Christians, as they partake of the bread and the cup, actually eat the *literal* body of Christ and drink His blood; or do they only eat and drink that which *symbolizes* the body and blood of Christ?

There is surely only one scriptural, sane, and satisfactory answer to this question. The believer, as he takes the bread and the cup discerns the body of Christ, in a *spiritual* way. He apprehends, by faith, the reality of that which the symbol sets forth. Thus he sees, in the loaf and the cup, a picture, symbol or figure of the body and blood of His blessed Lord and Savior.

In the light of that which Scripture plainly reveals, he discerns or apprehends the deep spiritual significance that lies behind the bread and the cup: the body and blood of Christ. From the Word of God he learns that this body was prepared in incarnation (Heb. 10:5-10). It was conceived by the Holy Spirit (Luke 1:30-35). It was born of a virgin (Matt. 1:18-23). It was sinlessly perfect in manifestation, for Christ was "holy, harmless, undefiled, separate from sinners" (Heb. 7:26). Absolute Deity and perfect Humanity were thus combined in His blessed Person (Isa. 9:6). It was offered as a substitutionary sacrifice for our sins, for they were "borne in His body on the tree" (1 Peter 2:24). It was raised in triumph from the grave and handled in resurrection (Luke 24:36-43). It is now glorious in the power of an endless life, at the right hand of the majesty on high (Luke 24:50-53; Acts 1:9-11; Heb. 7:16).

All the blessed reality of this greatest of all transactions is thus set forth in the simplicity and profundity of the Lord's supper. The more one's mind is allowed to dwell upon this ordinance, and the One who instituted it, the more he will be enabled to appreciate the deep spiritual significance of what is involved in "discerning the Lord's body."

We shall examine four main interpretations of these words of our Savior and seek to discover, in the light of the general teaching of Scripture, which of them is correct. We are assured that "God hath not given us the spirit of fear; but of power, and of love, and of a sound mind" (2 Tim. 1:7). God does not rob a Christian of his common sense, nor of his powers of reason, but appeals to both, and seeks to enlighten them by the revelation He has given us in His Word.

Notice the above expression: "the general teaching of the Word of God." Almost any false theory, invented by man, can find *apparent* support in an isolated verse of the Bible; but when this theory is examined in the light of *all the other Scriptures* referring to this particular subject, its falsity will become evident. Hence the absolute necessity for interpreting any Scripture in the light of all the Scriptures. The best commentary on the Bible is the Bible! Each Christian must emulate the example of those of Berea who "received the Word with all readiness of mind, and searched the Scriptures daily, whether these things were so" (Acts 17:11).

We shall first examine the Roman Catholic theory, which is called *Transubstantiation*. Then we shall consider the Lutheran theory, which is called *Consubstantiation*. Next we shall think of the Reformed view, sometimes called *Impanation*, which was the idea of Calvin. Finally, we shall state what we believe to be the Scriptural view.

1. Transubstantiation

This is the view held by a great religious organization, the Roman Catholic Church, that has many millions of adherents. The meaning of the word "transubstantiation" is defined for us by the Council of Trent, (AD 1551). This reads as follows: "By the consecration of the bread and wine, the entire substance of the bread is converted into the substance of the body of Christ, our Lord; and the entire substance of wine into the substance of His blood, which conversion is, by the Catholic Church, fittingly and rightly termed Transubstantiation."

Cyril of Jerusalem (AD 386), in his catechism, states concerning the bread and the wine, after its consecration by the priest: "Judge not by the taste, but by faith; put away hesitation, and be certain that ye have been honored with the gift of the body and blood of Christ. Taught thus; imbued with this most sure faith, that what seems bread is not bread—though to the taste it may seem so—but is the body of Christ; that what seems wine is not wine—though to the sense it may seem to be so—but the blood of Christ—in this faith strengthen thy heart."

In this same Council of Trent, the further statement was made: "If any man shall say that in the most holy sacrament of the Eucharist there remains the substance of wine, together with the body and blood of our Lord Jesus Christ, and shall deny the marvelous and unique conversion of the entire substance of the bread into His body, and of the entire substance of the wine into His blood, while the species of bread and wine alone remain, a conversion which the Catholic Church fittingly terms Transubstantiation, let him be anathema (accursed)." Thus a solemn curse was pronounced upon all who dared to deny this monstrous theory.

This shameful travesty of the simple ordinance of the Lord's supper did not come suddenly, but was the result of a gradual introduction of various theories which culminated in the doctrine of the Mass. In fact, it didn't become an *established* doctrine until the ninth century, though it was taught for many years before. The catacombs of Rome, which were closed in AD 300, contain no reference to the celebration of the Mass, showing it was not in existence at that time.

Neander, the historian, has recorded the theory of transubstantiation thus: "The idea of a sacrifice in the supper of our Lord was at first barely symbolical . . . but as one error begets another, it was quite natural that the notion of a particular priesthood in the Christian Church, corresponding to that in the Old Testament, should give birth to that of the notion of a sacrificial worship in the New Testament, which should stand in a similar relation to that of the Old Testament. So it came about that the whole idea of sacrifice in the Lord's supper, which in the first instance was simply symbolical, took a direction altogether wide of its true import, the earliest of which we find in Cyprian" (Born about AD 200).

Christendom today is very largely a mixture of Judaism and Paganism. The ritual, customs, and traditions of both have been introduced into Christianity. The result is a horrible hodge-podge, far removed and utterly distinct from the pattern revealed in the New Testament. One may well ask, when entering one of their so-called "places of worship": Whence came all these gaudy vestments; these tinkling bells; these burning candles; this smoking incense; these crosses; this bloodless altar, this ornate ritual, with the sing-song intonation of its readymade prayers, and the ordered responses of the congregation; and this unholy distinction between clergy and laity? By what authority have they been introduced? Have they a Divine origin and a Scriptural foundation? The answer is a most emphatic negative. They are the results of man-made expediency, which has substituted the inventions of men for the scriptural and spiritual worship which God's Word so clearly indicates.

We must beware of basing our *authority* for Church truth on the Old Testament, for the truth of the Church is exclusively a New Testament revelation, and entirely distinct from Judaism. There is no mention of the Church in the Old Testament. In fact, we are definitely told that the Church was a mystery (that is, a hitherto unrevealed secret), "which in other ages was not made known unto the sons of men, as it is now revealed unto His holy apostles and prophets by the Spirit" (Eph. 3:3-6).

However, the Old Testament may well be used to illustrate some truth which is clearly taught in the New Testament, for the Old Testament has been aptly termed, "the picture book of the New Testament." It was the failure to recognize this fact that led the early Church fathers to incorporate into the Church what belonged exclusively to Judaism, all of which was done away by the sacrifice of Christ.

The tendency of the flesh, in man, is to turn a simple ordinance of Scripture into a complex ritual, by adding various ideas and interpretations to what the Word of God has plainly revealed. When man attempts to "improve" upon the Divine pattern, it always ends disastrously, as is demonstrated in the Roman Church.

Rome bases its claim for the theory of transubstantiation on a literal interpretation of our Lord's words, "This is My body . . .This is My blood." They point out that Christ did not say: "This is the *symbol* of My body and My blood" or, "This *represents* My body and My blood," but He distinctly and plainly declared: This *is* My body . . . This *is* My blood." The answer to this argument is quite simple. We have only to examine this statement in the light of other similar statements which Christ made, to see the absurdity of their contention.

For instance, Christ said: "I am the true vine" (John 15:1). Did He w to convey to His disciples that He was a *literal* grape vine? He said: "I am the door" (John 10:9). Did He mean that He was *literally* and actually a wooden door? Of course not. He simply used the words "vine" and "door" in a figurative sense. The Bible abounds in such metaphorical language. A metaphor is a figure of speech in which one object is likened unto another object by asserting that it is the other object. For instance, we say of a man that "he fought *like* a lion in the battle." This is a similie, which is usually denoted by the word, "like." If we say: "He *was a lion* in the battle," this is a metaphor. Instead of likening him to a lion we have declared he *was* a lion.

Let us take a few of these metaphors, and see how absurd it would be to take them literally. "The seven candlesticks are seven churches" (Rev. 1:20). Were these churches literal candles, or were they likened to candles in that they gave light to those around? "The seven heads are seven mountains" (Rev. 17:9). Were these heads actually mountains, or were they likened unto mountains? "These two women are two covenants" (Gal. 4:24). Were these two women, Sarah and Hagar, actually covenants, or did they *represent* two covenants? There are many other such metaphors in the Word of God, that are not intended to be taken literally, but only to be understood *figuratively*.

We are constantly using such figurative language in our daily speech. For instance: we are invited to the home of a Christian. As we enter, we notice a photograph of a lady hanging on the wall. When we inquire of our host, "Who is that?" he replies, "That is my mother." Now did he wish us to understand that his mother was a photograph, or did he mean that the photograph was a picture, or representation of his mother! Sometimes a person will show us a photograph of a house and say, "This is my house." Does he mean that he lived in that photograph, or that the photograph is merely a likeness of the house in which he lives? So when Christ said, "This is My body, 'This is My blood," He simply meant "This is the *symbol* of My body and blood."

As C. F. Hogg has pointed out: "The words actually used are capable of two meanings: either that the object is what it is described to be; or that the object *represents* that which it is said to be. That in this case (that is, the words of Christ, "This is My body") the former is not intended is evident, if only from the obvious fact that the bread, of which Christ spoke, was actually held in His hand, which was part of His body, and altogether separate and distinct from that which it held. Did they understand Him to mean that the bread was His body, and that the Lord at that moment had two bodies? To ask the question seems a sufficient answer. The alternative then will be the true interpretation of the words, as it is the obvious one: 'This bread *represents* My body.'"

When Christ broke and ate that bread, was He eating His own body, or did He only eat that which symbolized His body? When He drank of the cup, was He drinking His own blood, or was He drinking that which symbolized His blood? The answer is surely obvious. When the disciples took the bread and ate it, and the cup and drank it, were they actually eating the literal body of Christ, and drinking His literal blood? If so, then they were guilty of cannibalism! Such a thought is as abhorrent as it is ridiculous. The Scripture narrative makes it quite plain. We are told that "Jesus took bread and blessed and brake it" (Mark 14:22). It does not say He took His body, or He took His blood, but simply the bread and the cup. The only sane explanation is that these *represented* His body and blood.

Our Lord declared emphatically: "Think not that I am come to destroy the law, or the prophets: I am not come to destroy but to fulfil" (Matt. 5:17). The law, which Christ came to fulfil, had declared that on no account must blood be eaten. It was absolutely forbidden. (See Lev. 3:17; 7:26; 17:14; Deut. 12:16; 12:23; 15:23.) Thus if Christ had given them His literal blood, He would have broken the very law He declared He had come to fulfil!

A good illustration of the graphic use of metaphor is found in 2 Samuel 23. The Philistines were in possession of the town of Bethlehem, while David was in the cave of Adullam. Being thirsty, David said: "O that one would give me drink of the water of the well of Bethlehem, which is by the gate!" Hearing this, three of his mighty men of valor broke through the ranks of the Philistines and brought to their master the water he desired. To David's credit, however, he would not taste a drop of that water, but poured it out before the Lord and said: "Be it far from me, O Lord, that I should do this: is not this the blood of the men that went in jeopardy of their lives?" Now, was it water or blood that David poured out before the Lord? Of course, it was only water, but he called it blood, because it had been secured at the risk of the lives of those brave men. Notice, he did not say: "This water is like blood," but he declared: "Is not this the blood of these men?"

Rome actually asserts that when Christ gave His disciples the bread and the cup, He actually gave them His literal body and blood in sacrifice, or, as they express it: "He *victimized* Himself." Thus, according to them, the *upper room*, and not *Calvary*, was the place of His sacrifice! The cross simply made this sacrifice of the upper room a public act! What a monstrous travesty of the Scripture revelation of the sacrifice of Christ!

A friend of mine, traveling by train, found himself seated next to an episcopal bishop, of the very high Church. The conversation turned on the subject of the Lord's supper and the meaning of our Savior's words: "This is My body." The bishop was most emphatic in his assertion that the bread and wine was actually the body and blood of Christ, and kept repeating: "But Jesus said: 'This is My body.' He did not say, 'This represents My body.'"

My friend suddenly gripped the bishop's thigh and exclaimed: "Well, this is the first time I knew you were made of grass!" "What do you mean?" inquired the surprised prelate. My friend replied: "The Bible says, 'All flesh is grass.' Of course you believe that to be a literal statement, don't you? It doesn't say 'All flesh is *like* grass,' but 'All flesh *is* grass'" (Isa. 40:6-8). The bishop had no more to say on this subject!

It is interesting to note that where this verse is quoted in the New Testament we read: "All flesh is as grass" (1 Peter 1:24). By this, of course, is meant that man's frailty is likened to grass which withereth. It also indicates that Peter was aware that the statement was not to be taken literally.

Romanists are fond of quoting the cryptic statement of our Lord as found in John 6:53, where we read: "Except ye eat the flesh of the Son of Man and drink His blood, ye have no life in you." They seek to apply these words to bolster their argument for their false theory of transubstantiation. The answer to this is quite simple. *This statement of our Lord has nothing whatever to do with the Lord's supper*, for this was not instituted until many months later. It simply refers, in symbolic language, to the believer's spiritual appropriation of Christ by believing on Him.

In John 6:35 Christ declared: "I am the Bread of life: he that cometh to Me shall never hunger; and he that believeth on Me shall never thirst." As by eating, we satisfy our natural hunger, and by drinking, gratify our natural thirst; so by coming to Christ our spiritual hunger is satisfied, and by believing on Him our spiritual thirst is quenched. Notice and compare vs. 54 with 47. "Whoso eateth My flesh and drinketh My blood hath eternal life." Thus eternal life, in symbolic language, is conditioned by eating His flesh and drinking His blood.

Now turn to verse 47, where the condition for the possession of eternal life is again stated, this time in plain language: "He that believeth on Me hath eternal life." Thus *believing on Him,* and *eating His flesh mean the same thing.* When a person believes on Christ, he thus appropriates Him, is united to Him, and is described in Scripture as being "in Christ" and Christ is in him. We could multiply Scriptures to prove this, but two will have to be sufficient: 2 Corinthians 5:17; John 15:5.

Even the disciples were puzzled by these words. (See John 6:51-52, 60-63.) They failed to realize that Christ was speaking in parabolic language, but the Lord explained His use of this metaphor by saying: "It is the Spirit that quickeneth: the flesh profiteth nothing: the words that I speak unto you, they are *spirit* and they are *life.*" It is a sound principle, in order to discover the real meaning of a statement of Scripture, to interpret what is difficult, obscure and debatable in the light of other Scriptures, relating to the same subject, which are simple, clear and definite in their meaning. Thus that which is obscure should not be allowed to contradict that which is clear.

The theory of transubstantiation, therefore, has *no support whatever* in the Word of God, which is the Christian's sole authority. It is wholly an invention of men. The reading of a reliable "Church History" will indicate how this idea came to be introduced and finally developed into the sacrifice of the Mass. A good book on this subject is Andrew Miller's *Church History.*

After the death of the original band of apostles, gifted men arose who, doubtless motivated by a sincere desire to "improve" on the pattern of Christianity, introduced various innovations which they fondly hoped would contribute to the development of the Church, and further its influence in the world. These men are called "the fathers." They wrote considerably, and their writings have been preserved to us. These writings are called "the Patristic writings," from the Latin word, "pater," which means "father." In these writings we can trace the beginnings of the departure from the pattern given in the New Testament.

These men would get an idea, which would gradually develop into a theory. They would then search the Bible to discover if they could find any support for this theory. After a while they would find some isolated text which, to them, apparently gave some support to their theory. Then, by a misinterpretation of this text, they would incorporate their idea into the teaching of the Church. Thus, instead of *getting out* from the Bible their authority for the doctrines they taught; they *put their theories into the Bible*, and then made the Bible fit their particular theory! Thus they wrested the Scriptures "unto their own destruction." (See 2 Peter 3:16.)

This departure from the faith had been foretold by the apostle Paul many years before. Let us listen to his words: "I know this, that after my departing shall grievous wolves enter in among you, not sparing the flock. Also of your own selves shall men arise, speaking perverse things, to draw away disciples after them. Therefore watch, and remember, that by the space of three years I ceased not to warn every one night and day with tears. And now, brethren, I commend you to God, and to the word of His grace, which is able to build you up, and give you an inheritance among all them that are sanctified" (Acts 20:28-32). Notice to what Paul commended these believers, not to the teachings of the Church, but to the Word of God itself.

Rome accepts these Patristic writings as being of equal authority with the word of God. In fact, Rome has four sources of authority on which to base its dogmas. First, the holy Scriptures. Second, the Apocrypha. Third, the Patristic writings. Fourth, the interpretation of the Church, by which of course, they mean themselves. By this means, any theory, however wild, fanciful and false can be foisted on a credulous public, which must accept their findings, or else be excommunicated from their organization! This will explain how this lovely and simple ordinance has degenerated into the horrible and blasphemous sacrifice of the Mass.

To push the argument of Rome to the utmost extreme, it may be said by some that while what we have pointed out is undoubtedly true, it is not thereby absolutely proved that our interpretation is correct. To this we answer: if transubstantiation is meant, and it would be admitted by all that this would be a most unusual and special revelation, why is no further statement given here, or anywhere else in Scripture, to back it up? Absolutely none whatever is found.

This false theory of transubstantiation, therefore, has *absolutely no foundation whatever* in the Word of God. It affirms that each time the Mass is celebrated, Christ is again sacrificed on its bloodless altar; and this, of course, is in direct contradiction to the plain teaching of the Word, which declares that "This Man, (Christ) after He had offered one sacrifice for sins forever, sat down on the right hand of God" (Heb. 10:12). As for such a person as an "officiating priest," the New Testament knows nothing about him. Every true believer has been constituted a priest unto God, and therefore may "offer up spiritual sacrifices, acceptable to God by Jesus Christ" (1 Peter 2:5).

George Goodman, in his excellent book, *Some Scriptural Principles*, relates an incident which serves to show the terrible lengths to which Rome goes in its false theory. He describes how a Christian man went into the Roman cathedral at Westminster (London), having in mind a desire to put a certain question to someone in authority there. He accordingly addressed himself to a priest whom he met walking across the building: "I believe that the teaching of your Church is that, at the words of consecration, the matter of the elements undergoes a miraculous change, and is converted into the very body and blood of our Lord Jesus Christ?" "That is so," replied the priest: "Christ Himself then descends on the altar. He is there 'propria persona,' as we say." "You mean that Christ is actually there, as truly as my arm is in the sleeve of my coat?" inquired the man. "Yes," replied the priest.

"Well, that is not my faith," remarked the visitor, "But this was the question I was desirous to ask you: When you have the Lord Jesus Christ upon your altars, and actually in your hands, what do you do with Him? Do you profess to put Him to death?" The priest answered, "Yes." The man persisted: "Do you profess to slay Him, to immolate and kill Jesus Christ upon your altars?" The priest seemed momentarily off his guard, but the dogma of his Church, as defined by the Council of Trent states that: 'His flesh, bones, nerves and divinity, under the accidents of bread and wine, are there.' Again the visitor put the question to the priest: "Do you put Him to death?" Again the priest was perforce to reply, "Yes."

The visitor then delivered his parting thrust: "If you profess to put Jesus Christ to death in the sacrifice of the Mass, do you not see that you crucify Him afresh, and thus declare yourselves as the successors of those on whom Peter himself charged the crime: 'Ye killed the Prince of Life' and whom Stephen called: 'His betrayers and murderers?'" This ended the conversation. It serves to show where such teaching leads, when once error is received.

One of the first points of departure, in the early church, was the rise and development of a special priesthood, which was not common to all believers. Certain men, because of their ability, were selected, ordained, and then placed in charge of a congregation of Christians. This meant that most, if not all the oral ministry was controlled by them. Thus priestcraft began to show its ugly head. Then came infant baptism, from which emerged the doctrine of baptismal regeneration. In the track of this came the idea that the Lord's supper should be viewed as a sacrifice. Borrowing from the ritual of the Aaronic priesthood, an altar was erected, vestments for the priests were designed. A prescribed order of service was prepared, complete with a carefully planned liturgy, in which certain prayers were recited, together with specified motions of the body. The sign of the cross was introduced, the use of incense and even idols were erected, before which they bowed. All this was done without any authority whatever from the Word of God.

These innovations were at first firmly resisted, but gradually opposition gave way to tolerance, and tolerance to apathy, and thus the "new order" was established and came to be looked upon as being "scriptural." This should come as a warning to all believers in this present day, for the Scriptures are being wrested to support all sorts of theories that have no foundation in the general teaching of the Word of God. Isaiah's words are very much to the point: "To the law and the testimony: if they speak not according to this word, they have no light in them" (Isa. 8:20). To this we may well quote the inspired words of Paul: "Prove all things, hold fast that which is good" (1 Thess. 5:21).

To sum up this rather long section. We unhesitatingly reject the theory of transubstantiation for the following good reasons:

(a) It denies the eternal efficacy of the one sacrifice which Christ offered, once and for all, and by which He has forever satisfied every claim of a holy God against the believing sinner. It is a sacrifice that will *never be repeated.*

(b) Our Lord did not intend His disciples to understand that it was His literal body and blood that He was giving them at the supper.

(c) The disciples did not so understand it, for in their writings, given by divine inspiration, there is no suggestion or support for the doctrine of transubstantiation.

(d) By the celebration of the Mass, Rome claims that Christ is re-sacrificed upon their altars each time the ceremony is performed. Thus they "crucify to themselves the Son of God afresh, and put Him to an open shame" (Heb. 6:6).

(e) The taking of the bread and cup has no saving virtue in it. The same is true of the ordinance of baptism. These ordinances were only intended for those who are already saved, justified, and "accepted in the Beloved."

(f) It is opposed to the "sound mind" which God has given to His people. It is good to know that "while faith is always *unreasoning*, it is never *unreasonable*."

(g) It is contrary to the general teaching of the New Testament Scriptures. Its only support is found *outside* the pages of holy writ, and this has no authority for the child of God.

We have spent some considerable time investigating this false theory, but we trust that what has been said will clarify the mind of the reader regarding this monstrous degradation of the beautiful ordinance that our Lord instituted.

Chapter Nine

The Purpose of the Lord's Supper:
Discerning the Body of Christ; Consubstantiation, Impanation, Memorial, Bread and Wine

2. Consubstantiation

Now let us turn our attention to another theory, also widely held, and this time by Protestants. This idea originated with the great Martin Luther at the time of the Reformation, early in the 16th century, Luther "renounced the Roman doctrine of transubtantiation, that the bread and wine after consecration remained no longer, but were changed into the material body and blood of Christ. Luther's idea was that the bread and wine remained just what they were before—real bread and real wine—but that there was also, together with the bread and wine, the material substances of Christ's human body" (Miller's *Church History*).

According to this peculiar theory, people who partook of the bread and the wine participated truly of the body and blood of Christ, in with, and under the bread and wine. He held that after the prayer of consecration, while the bread and wine remained unchanged, yet, in some mysterious way, Christ was communicated to the partaker, whether he was a believer or not. He denied that the Lord's supper was a sacrifice, or that the body of Christ in the elements was to be worshipped; but he maintained that the body of Christ was there nevertheless, and was received by the communicant.

It is a difficult theory to define, for it abounds in terms that are practically inexplicable. Someone has tried to illustrate this peculiar view by likening the bread and wine to a poker which has been placed in a fire. After a while, it will be observed that not only is the poker in the fire, but that now the fire is also in the poker. Thus, in some mystical and magical fashion, after the consecration of the elements by the clergyman, the body and blood of Christ is in the bread and wine.

It has been expressed thus, "The body of Christ, in accordance of the will and omnipotence of God and its own ubiquity, is really and substantially present, in with and under the supper, even as His divine nature is in the human, and as warmth is in the fire. Wherefore the supper is physically partaken of by those who are unworthy, albeit to their own destruction." Luther's insistence on this peculiar view caused a division in Protestantism.

At a conference in Marburg in October 1529, Luther met Ulrich Zwingle, the great Swiss reformer, in public debate on this question. The first thing Luther did, on entering the room, was to write on the table in front of him, in Latin, the words, "Hoc est corpus meum," or, "This is my body." To these words he constantly returned when Zwingle, by his superior scriptural arguments, forced Luther into a corner. He declared, "Christ said, 'This is My body.' Let them show me that a body is not a body. I rejected reason, common sense, carnal arguments and mathematical proofs. God is above mathematics. We have the Word of God; we must adore and perform it!" From this position Luther refused to budge, and thus the breach between these two great men remained.

Needless to say, we unhesitatingly reject this theory of consubtantiation, and for the same reason that we rejected transubstantiation—it has no scriptural support. Apparently Luther was never able to divest himself of all the grave clothes of Rome. In attempting to avoid the dreadful error of transubstatiation, he fell into the error of inventing a theory of his own, which also lacked the support of the plain teaching of Scripture.

While we thank God for the Reformation, and for the recovery of the great truth of justification by faith which Luther fearlessly proclaimed; yet we must deplore his failure to see and teach the scriptural truth concerning the spiritual meaning of the Lord's supper as a simple memorial of Christ. While we do not doubt his sincerity for a moment, yet we must conclude that he was sincerely mistaken, and this is a tragedy indeed.

3. The Reformed view, sometimes called Impanation

Calvin was one of the great intellectuals of the Reformation. While he rejected transubstatiation and consubstatiation, he could not wholly divest himself of the idea that some spiritual virtue was in the elements. He taught that the communicant receives Christ, who is spiritually present in the elements, but only by faith. He declared that though the flesh of Christ is in heaven, the Holy Spirit unites it with the bread and wine. Again there is a difficulty in defining this theory, for its wording is so vague. In his "Institutes," he states his theory concerning the Lord's supper as follows: "That sacred communion of flesh and blood, by which Christ transfuses His life in us, just as if it penetrated our bones and marrow, He testifies and seals in the Supper, and that not by presenting a vain and empty sign, but by these exerting an efficacy of the Spirit by which He fulfils what He promises." One would gather from these words that Calvin believed that all those who partake of the Lord's supper, in true faith, received the blessings of salvation.

Again we must reject this very involved and highly fanciful theory, for it also has no support in the clear teaching of the New Testament. This plainly affirms that the Lord's supper is but a simple, yet very beautiful and spiritually significant *memorial* of the Lord Jesus.

4. A Memorial of Christ

Let us now look at the fourth view, which we believe to be the scriptural one, and which we shall call "a memorial of Christ." In what way does a believer "discern the body of Christ," as he partakes of the Lord's supper? The answer is quite scriptural, simple, sane and satisfactory; he discerns it *spiritually*. He realizes that the loaf and the cup are only the divinely appointed *emblems*, symbols or pictures which *illustrate* the reality they combine to show forth, namely, the sacrifice of the body and blood of Christ. In other words, the believer knows that there is no saving virtue whatever in the bread and wine. Their value lies only in enabling him to spiritually apprehend what they convey to his mind, the sacrifice of Christ which need not, and indeed, cannot be repeated.

> Only bread and only wine,
> Yet to faith the solemn sign
> Of the heavenly and divine;
> We give Thee thanks, O Lord.
>
> (H. Bonar)

As the Christian takes the bread he says, as it were: "Lord Jesus, I take this bread as the symbol of Thy body, in the which Thou didst bear my sins, take my place and die in my stead. In glad obedience to Thy request, I eat this bread in remembrance of Thee." As he takes the cup, he says, as it were: "Lord Jesus, this is the symbol of Thy precious blood which Thou didst shed for my redemption. I take it, as from Thyself, in fond and grateful remembrance of Thee." Thus humbly, reverently and adoringly, he receives the bread and the cup. In this way, he fulfils the purpose the Lord had in instituting the supper: "This do for a remembrance of Me." How simple, yet how impressive is such a scriptural observance of the Lord's supper!

The proper observance of the Lord's supper, therefore, calls for spiritual intelligence and discernment on the part of the partaker. It is not a mere mechanical rite that enables a person to go through certain motions, without any exercise of heart and mind. Such a mechanical rite is completely without necessity, and entirely uncalled for in Scripture. It tends to give the partaker, in his own mind, a totally unwarranted satisfaction of having done something good and meritorious.

The believers at Corinth had failed to realize the purpose of the supper, and this had brought upon them the chastening hand of God. We, too, must beware of approaching the Lord's supper in a careless and indifferent manner. We must ever realize that we are there at the invitation of the Lord of glory, and that Christ Himself, though unseen, is present as the Host at His own supper, and that the purpose of the supper is to remember Him in a worthy manner by spiritually discerning, in the elements, the Lord's body.

Lord Jesus, in Thy precious name,
And in that name alone;
At Thy request we gladly meet,
Thy Lordship here would own.

As on that dark, betrayal night,
Thou didst this feast ordain;
We too, the bread and cup would take,
Thy death, Lord, thus proclaim.

The bread, Thy body doth portray;
The cup, Thy precious blood;
By which our sin was put away,
Our peace was made with God.

The Host art Thou, O blessed Lord,
Thy honored guests are we;
With grateful and adoring hearts
We would remember Thee!

Lord Jesus, Whom, unseen, we love,
As thus we muse on Thee;
We none would see, save Thee alone,
Thou Man of Calvary!

5. A word as to the kind of bread and wine

The question is often raised as to what kind of bread and wine should be used at the supper. Should it be leavened or unleavened bread? Should it be fermented or unfermented wine? The answer is, Scripture has nothing to say regarding this matter, and where the Word of God is silent, we do well to follow its example! Some strong minded individuals, with a legalistic and ritualistic turn of mind, have attempted to introduce this question into an assembly. The resultant controversy, together with the inevitable heat gendered by the friction, has sometimes resulted in a division. It reminds one of the story of the little village council that met in solemn conclave to discuss the question as to what color they should whitewash the village pump!

The wise words of that veteran preacher, John Wesley, are worthy of our earnest and sober consideration: "What the Bible commands is good. What the Bible forbids is evil. What the Bible neither commands nor forbids, either in plain words or in undeniable evidence, is a thing in itself indifferent, and neither good nor evil. The Bible is our sole guide, and our adequate guide in faith and conduct."

Doubtless, though we are not specifically told, the bread our Lord used at the supper was unleavened bread, for it was used after the Passover feast. The reason for this is obvious: it was the *only bread available at that time.* Had there been any spiritual significance, or doctrinal importance involved in the kind of bread used, surely the Lord would have drawn our attention to this fact at the time. Many years later, the apostle Paul received a special revelation from the glorified Lord in regard to the Lord's supper; but again, there is *no mention whatever* in this revelation, as to what *kind* of bread should be used. Surely, if this was an important matter, the Lord would have indicated this fact to His servant.

Paul refers to the "feast" (holyday) in 1 Corinthians 5:8, but this has no reference to the Lord's supper. This feast refers to the whole period of the believer's life. The reference to leaven has to do with sin in the assembly, from which they are exhorted to purge themselves.

What is true of the bread is also true of the wine. No mention is made as to whether it should be fermented or unfermented. The degree of fermentation could be controlled by those who made it. In fact, the actual word, "wine," is not used at all. Christ spoke of it as "the fruit of the vine" (Luke 22:18). Doubtless the kind of wine used by the believers in Corinth was fermented, for it caused some of them to be "drunken." In seeking to correct this disorder that prevailed, Paul was presented with an excellent opportunity to specify the kind of wine they should use which would prevent a recurrence of this shameful thing; but no, all he did was to emphasize the fact that the Lord's supper was not an ordinary meal, but an ordinance that existed for the sole purpose of the remembrance of Christ. Thus, in the New Testament, the *kind* of bread and wine is entirely immaterial.

Some years ago, a small group of missionaries were gathered together to remember the Lord at a mission station. As they were about to begin, a visitor called, who was a well known and highly respected Christian. He inquired of the senior missionary if it would be permissible for him to join them in the Lord's supper. He was assured that, knowing he was a child of God, sound in doctrine and moral in life, they would be glad to welcome him as a fellow guest. At this the visitor said: "Before I could consent to join you, I would like to know what kind of wine you use. If it is fermented wine, I couldn't possibly meet with you." The missionary replied: "We are not gathered here to a kind of wine, but we meet in the name of the Lord Jesus to remember Him. If you are gathered to a kind of wine, it might be best for you to sit out on the porch, while we go inside and remember the Lord Jesus!" They had no more difficulty with this brother!

We need to beware of any strong-minded individual, however sincere he may be, who attempts to force his own ideas on an assembly as to what *kind* of bread and wine should be used, and demands that unless this or that kind is used he will not remain in the assembly. An assembly would be far better off without such a man. To grant such a person an inch will soon result in him demanding a yard, and the assembly will eventually be brought into legalistic bondage, and thus turned aside from the "simplicity which is in Christ."

A fanatic has been aptly defined as: "A person who majors on a minor." Some people live for nothing else than to take an inconsequental thing, magnify it out of all proportion to its spiritual importance, and make it a burning issue. These individuals are never happier than when they are splitting hairs, except when they are able to resplit the split hair, and so on, ad nauseum.

Chapter Ten

The Purpose of the Lord's Supper:
Proclamation, Anticipation

The Proclamation of the Lord's Death

The third purpose of the Lord's supper is the proclamation of the Lord's death. We read, "As often as ye eat this bread and drink this cup ye do show ("proclaim" R.V.) the Lord's death till He come" (1 Cor. 11:26). The word translated, "show," is the same word in the original which is translated "Preach," in Acts 4:2; 13:5, 38; 15:36; 17:3, 13; 1 Corinthians 9:14; Philippians 1:16, 18; Colossians 1:28. Thus, at the Lord's supper, the great central fact of the gospel, the death of Christ, is proclaimed in no uncertain way. In other words, Christians do not come together to "*remember* the Lord's death," but to *proclaim* it. They meet to remember His *Person*, and break the bread and drink the cup to *proclaim* His *passion*. It is good to distinguish between these two things. To whom do Christians proclaim the Lord's death?

1. The believer proclaims it to himself

Each time he partakes of the elements, he reminds himself that, but for the death of Christ on his behalf, he would still be in his sins, lost, guilty and undone. As, on the table, he sees the bread and the cup separated from each other, he realizes that this speaks eloquently of the death of his Divine Substitute who, by His death, satisfied every claim of a holy law, and every demand of a holy God on his behalf. Thus, each Lord's day, the believer is brought back to the great fundamental fact of the gospel, and the vital truth of Christianity, the death of Christ. As he takes the bread and the cup, he says, in effect: "Lord Jesus, but for Thy death on my behalf, I would still be dead in my trespasses and sins, and on my way to a lost eternity. I hereby confess that my present salvation and my future blessedness is due entirely to Thy death for me."

Doubtless this is one of the reasons why companies of believers, who seek to meet in a scriptural manner to remember the Lord Jesus each Lord's day, have been kept from serious doctrinal error. As they take the Lord's supper each week, they are brought back to the great foundation truth of the gospel: the substitutionary sacrifice of the Son of God on their behalf. Thus Calvary is ever kept fresh in their minds.

2. The believer proclaims it to the world

Since the word, "katangello," translated "show," means to preach, and preaching is the God-ordained means of making known the truth of the gospel; so the Lord's supper proclaims to the world, and to any unsaved person who may be present at the supper, the greatest event in the history of the universe, the death of Christ. His death is the record of the greatest love ever shown by God to man, and the greatest crime ever committed by man against God.

Many an unsaved person, as he has viewed the observance of the Lord's supper has, by this pictorial means, been convicted of his need of a Savior and led to trust the One whose death for him has thus been proclaimed to him. As he has read and sung the hymns which have been announced, heard the expressions of praise and worship from one and another of the brethren, and listened to a message from the Word of God, he has been impressed with the great truth of the Person and work of the Son of God. Then, as he has witnessed the breaking of the bread and the drinking of the cup, he has been led to put his faith in the Lord Jesus and to enter into the blessedness of the one whose "sins are forgiven" (Ps. 32:1-2).

The Lord Jesus, by instituting this supper, thus made certain that, in a world that rejected and despised Him, there should be this weekly proclamation of His death. Each person who rejects, despises, or neglects Christ as his Savior, by this very attitude, takes sides with those who, long ago, cried: "Away with Him . . . Let Him be crucified!" This is the great crime with which the world is charged. All who come to Christ, and trust Him as their Savior, are cleared from that charge and declared to be justified in the sight of God (Rom. 5:1). Thus, each time the Lord's supper is observed, this glorious truth is proclaimed. The poet has expressed it thus:

> No gospel like this feast,
> Spread for the Church by Thee;
> Nor prophets nor evangelists
> Preach the glad news more free;

All our redemption cost,
  All Thy redemption won;
All it has won for us, the lost,
  All it cost Thee, the Son.

Thine was the bitter price,
  Ours is the free gift given;
Thine was the blood of sacrifice,
  Ours is the wine of heaven.
(Mrs. Rundle Charles)

3. The believer announces it, in a sense, to the principalities and powers in the heavenlies

There is a tremendous statement found in Paul's letter to the Ephesians which reads: "And to make all men see what is the fellowship of the mystery, which from the beginning of the world hath been hid in God, who created all things by Jesus Christ: to the intent that now unto the principalities and powers in heavenly places might be known, by the Church, the manifold wisdom of God according to the eternal purpose which He purposed in Christ Jesus, our Lord" (Eph. 3:9-11). By this we learn that the Church on earth is God's object lesson to those spirit beings that form the principalities and powers in the heavenlies. Since this is so, then they, too, as they see companies of believers meeting in the name of their Lord and Creator rejoice as they thus see the wondrous truth of His death proclaimed.

This is one of the reasons given why women should have their heads covered in the assembly: "Because of the angels" (1 Cor. 11:10). The unfallen angels are greatly interested in the gospel which was the subject of the prophetic writings of old time. These prophets, who "spake as they were moved by the Holy Spirit," recorded the very words of God, and "testified beforehand the sufferings of Christ, and the glory that should follow . . . which things the angels desire to look into" (2 Peter 1:21; 1 Peter 1:10-12).

These angelic beings saw Him as the Babe of Bethlehem, the Carpenter of Nazareth, the tempted Man in the wilderness, the Man of Sychar's well, the lonely Man in the garden, the despised Man in the Judgment Hall, and the forsaken Man of Calvary. They had announced His triumphant resurrection and witnessed His glorious ascension, and they now surround the throne and joyously fulfil His will. What joy, therefore, must be theirs as they view thousands of Christians proclaiming the Lord's death as they partake of the Lord's supper!

And what shall be said of those fallen angels, with Satan as their leader, as they are reminded, through this proclamation, of the death of Christ? It was through this death that Christ destroyed "him that had the power of death, that is, the Devil" (Heb. 2:14-15). Satan's doom has been pronounced and, in our Lord's good time, the sentence imposed will be carried out (Rev. 20:10). Satan well realizes this fact, and has therefore sought to bury the real spiritual significance of the Lord's supper beneath the rubbish of sacerdotalism, ritualism, formalism and human tradition. Alas, he has only been too successful in his evil task!

The Anticipation of the Lord's Coming

The Lord's supper, as we have seen, is a *temporary* thing. There is a time coming when believers will no longer need the bread and the cup to remind them of the Lord Jesus, for they shall be with Him and "behold His face" (Rev. 22:4). The Lord's supper not only allows the believer to look *backward* to Calvary to see Him crucified, and *upward* to heaven to see Him glorified; but he can also look *forward* to the time when "He that shall come will come," and take all His people to that home He has prepared for them (John 14:1-3). Thus anticipation is no small part of the Lord's supper. Each time believers take the bread and the cup, it may be for the last time. Perhaps by the next Lord's day they shall be all together in His presence, to go no more out.

What a wealth of meaning is found in those three little monosyllables: "Till He come!" This literal and personal return of the Lord Jesus is the hope of the Church as a whole, and of each believer in particular.

Another lovely illustration of this truth is found in the life of Joseph. As he neared the end of his life, he called his brethren around him and, in the role of a prophet said: "God will surely visit you, and bring you out of this land unto the land which He sware to Abraham, Isaac and Jacob." Then Joseph made them swear to him that they would not bury his body in the land of Egypt, but preserve it and carry it with them when God brought them out of the land of Egypt. Joseph then died and his body was embalmed and placed in a coffin in Egypt (Gen. 50:24-26). It is this incident that is selected in Hebrews chapter eleven, to illustrate the virtue of his faith (Heb. 11:22).

Faith presupposes a prior revelation, for we are told: "faith cometh by hearing, and hearing by the Word of God" (Rom. 10:17). Abraham had passed on this promise of God to his son Isaac, and Isaac gave it to Jacob, and Jacob to Joseph. It was therefore on the basis of this revelation that Joseph gave the commandment concerning the disposal of his bones.

Sixty-four years after Joseph's death, a new dynasty of kings arose in Egypt. The new king, seeing that the children of Israel had multiplied exceedingly, and fearing they would join forces with an enemy should it invade the land, decided on a bold stroke, and enslaved the whole nation of Israel. For many years he made their lives "bitter with hard bondage, in mortar and in brick, and in all manner of service in the field, all their service wherein they made them serve was with rigour" (Ex. 1:13-15). Egypt now became the land of bondage to the people of Israel. Their groans, cries and tears mingled with the taskmasters' whips, as they drove them to their tasks from early morning until evening.

During the entire period of their enslavement, however, there was a gleam of hope; the bones of Joseph were in their midst. Each time they looked upon the coffin, they were reminded that this bondage would not last for ever, and that one day God would visit them and take them to the land of promise. Sure enough, when God's time came, He raised up Moses to be their deliverer. Accompanied by a series of mighty miracles they were then emancipated from the slavery that had so long been their lot, and brought out, with a high hand, by their omnipotent God.

We are told that when Israel left the land they "took the bones of Joseph," and ultimately these bones were buried in the land of promise (Ex. 13:19; Josh. 24:32-33).

In like manner, Christians have, in the Lord's supper, that which points them forward to "the land that is fairer than day," into which they shall be brought at the second advent of the Lord Jesus Christ. They will then leave behind, forever, a groaning and travailing creation, and be introduced to a sphere where there is no more sin, pain, tears, sorrow, disappointment, darkness, disease or death. As the sight of the bones of Joseph cheered the enslaved people of Israel, so the bread and the cup assure Christians that the great deliverance day is coming, when our Lord shall appear for His people.

It is fitting, therefore, to sing that beautiful hymn which reminds us, each Lord's day, of the blessed moment when the silence of heaven shall be broken by the voice of Him, "whom, having not seen, we love."

Till He come, O let the words
   Linger on the trembling cords;
Let the 'little while' between
   In their golden light be seen;
Let us think how heaven and home
   Lie beyond that 'Till He come!'

Sweet the feast of love Divine,
   Broken bread and outpoured wine;
Sweet memorials till the Lord
   Calls us round His heavenly board,
Some from earth, from glory some,
   Severed only, 'Till He come.'

(E. H. Bickersteth)

Chapter Eleven

The Participants of the Lord's Supper:
Saved, Sound, Clean

Having dealt with the matter of the institution, the symbolism and the purpose of the Lord's supper, we now come to a consideration of its participants. Only one class of people are viewed in the New Testament as partaking of the Lord's supper. These are believers in the Lord Jesus Christ, who are doctrinally sound and morally clean. In other words, those who are heaven born, heaven bound and heaven bent. Let us now deal particularly with this phase of our subject.

The Participants Should be Genuinely Saved

This fact is seen at the institution of the supper. It was to His disciples that the Lord said: "This do for a remembrance of Me." Scripture does not contemplate a mixed multitude, composed of saved and unsaved, linked together in a common membership and participation in this holy ordinance. Scripture places, as it were, over the door leading to this supper a sign, which reads: "For believers only."

For this fact we have abundant evidence. We are told: "Then they that *gladly received his word* were baptized; and the same day there were added unto them about 3000 souls. And they continued stedfastly in the apostles' doctrine and fellowship, and in breaking of bread and in prayers" (Acts 2:41-42). We are informed that "Upon the first day of the week, when the disciples came together to break bread, Paul preached unto them" (Act 20:7). The letter which contains the revelation of the Lord's supper is addressed to: "The Church of God which is at Corinth, to them that are *sanctified in Christ Jesus*, called to be saints, with all that in every place call upon the name of Jesus Christ, our Lord, both theirs and ours" (1 Cor. 1:2). It was to such that Paul wrote: "The preaching of the cross is to them that perish, foolishness; but unto us which are saved, it is the power of God" (1 Cor. 1:18). Later on, these same people were assured: "But ye are washed, ye are sanctified, but ye are justified in the name of the Lord Jesus, and by the Spirit of our God" (1 Cor. 6:11). Thus these people, who partook of the Lord's supper, "belonged to Christ." See Mark 9:41; 1 Corinthians 3:23.

Believers in the Lord Jesus are variously described in the New Testament as, "brethren," "disciples," "saints," "Christians," "children of God" and "believers." Each title implies that the person so addressed has been regenerated by the Spirit of God upon his personal acceptance of Christ as Savior and Lord. Thus it is taken for granted that only true Christians are free to partake of the bread and the cup. It is Christians *only* who are described as being a "holy and a royal priesthood," and are thus divinely fitted to offer up "spiritual sacrifices, acceptable to God through Jesus Christ" our Lord (1 Peter 2:4-9).

In the early days of Christianity it was as much as a man's life was worth to name the name of Christ. Such a person was a marked man, and became the target for the world's scorn, shame, persecution, imprisonment and death. Christianity was not the popular thing that it is today. This persecution, however, had the good effect of separating the wheat from the chaff, and consequently a high standard of spirituality resulted from this weeding-out process. In fact, we are told: "And of the rest (that is, the unsaved) durst no man join himself unto them" (Acts 5:13). Each genuine Christian can be distinguished by three marks.

1. He is saved by the grace of God

To such Paul wrote: "For by grace are ye saved through faith . . . not of works, lest any man should boast" (Eph. 2:8, 9). A Christian is a person who has seen his need as a lost and guilty sinner, and has believed the gospel that Christ died for his sins and rose from the grave. He has personally rested in the finished work of Christ, and received Him as his own Savior, and confessed Him as the Lord of his life. God declares of all such that they are saved and secure eternally.

2. He is indwelt by the Spirit of God

The body of every believer is now the temple of God, for the Holy Spirit, by His indwelling presence, has "sealed him unto the day of redemption" (1 Cor. 6:19-20; Eph. 4:30). Not only is he indwelt by the Spirit, but there has been communicated to him a divine nature, in the strength of which he can now live a life well pleasing to his Lord. Moreover he is now enabled to love and understand the Word of God. Through his study of the Word, and prayer, plus witnessing about Christ to others, the Christian can now "grow in grace and in the knowledge of his Lord and Savior (2 Peter 1:3-8; 3:18).

3. He is obedient to the Word of God

The Christian has but one guide book, and that is the Bible. It will be to him "a lamp unto his feet and a light unto his path" (Ps. 119:105). As he humbly, reverently and believingly studies the Scriptures for himself, and obeys what he finds written therein, he will be led into paths pleasing to the Lord, and profitable to his own spiritual life. This, in turn, will enable him to be a blessing to others. May this three fold qualification be yours and mine!

The Participants Should be Doctrinally Sound

We are living in days characterized not only by the declension of spiritual life, but also by departure from the fundamental truths of our most holy faith. One of the marks of the "last days" is that many "Will not endure sound doctrine, but after their own lusts shall they heap to themselves teachers, having itching ears; and they shall turn away their ears from the truth, and shall be turned unto fables" (2 Tim. 4:3-4). The foundation truths of Christianity are being assailed on every hand, not only by atheists, agnostics and false cults, but also by those who have the temerity to call themselves Christians and, in many cases, actually occupy professedly Christian pulpits! In many denominations, these modernistic preachers outnumber those who are seeking to preach the truth! Thus, in Christendom, there exists this utter confusion of voices.

Needless to say, these men who deny the fundamental truths of the faith are not Christians at all, and should therefore not be permitted to partake of the Lord's supper, for they have "no part nor lot in this matter" (Acts 8:21). We are definitely told: "Whosoever transgresseth and abideth not in the doctrine of Christ . . . receive him not" (2 John 9-10). If such men are allowed to come into an assembly, they will soon ruin the testimony. The Scripture asks a question: "How can two walk together except they be agreed?" (Amos 3:3). Again the question is asked: "What part hath he that believeth with an infidel [an unbeliever]?" (2 Cor. 6:15).

Inasmuch as we shall be using the word "assembly" quite frequently from this point on, it may be well to define the term. By "assembly" is meant a company of genuine Christians, who gather together in the name of the Lord Jesus alone, for either prayer, praise and worship, or the study of the Word of God, or for the remembrance of the Lord Jesus in the breaking of bread, or for mutual edification. These groups of Christians are called "churches," or "assemblies" in the New Testament. Each Christian should seek to associate himself with such a scripturally gathered company of believers, and thus enjoy the privilege of fellowship with the people of God.

The New Testament has quite a little to say about "soundness." It speaks of "sound doctrine" (1 Tim. 1:10; 4:3; Titus 1:9). It describes "sound men" who are "sound in the faith" (Titus 1:13). These men are thus able "by sound doctrine both to exhort and convince the gainsayers" (Titus 1:9). It commends the use of "sound words," and of "sound speech that cannot be condemned" (2 Tim. 1:13; Titus 2:8).

Let us think, for a few moments, of some of these sound doctrines, which combine to form these foundation truths: the faith which was "once delivered unto the saints" (Jude 3). Briefly, we will name seven of them:

(1) The Bible is the divinely inspired word of God in every part, and is therefore absolutely authoritative on every subject dealt within its pages (2 Tim. 3:15-17).

(2) The essential and eternal Deity of our Lord Jesus Christ, as equal and eternal with the Father and the Holy Spirit. That He became incarnate by a virgin birth, and therefore combines in Himself absolute Deity and perfect and sinless humanity (1 Tim. 3:16; Col. 1:13-20; John 1:1-4).

(3) The necessity for and the eternal efficacy of Christ's substitutionary sacrifice: This, and His victorious resurrection, held as the sole basis of a sinner's acceptance with God (Rom. 3:24-26; 1 Cor. 15:1-8; John 3:14-18).

(4) The ruined state of all humanity by nature and man's need of regeneration ere he can see or enter the kingdom of God (John 3:1-7; Rom. 3:9-24).

(5) That salvation is wholly of grace, and therefore entirely apart from human merit. It is conditioned by repentance towards God, faith in the Person and work of the Son of God, and confession of Him as Lord of life (Eph. 2:1-10; Acts 20:20-21; Rom. 4:1-8, 11:6, 10:8-13).

(6) The Deity and personality of the Holy Spirit. That He inspired the Word of God, convicts the sinner of his need of salvation and, on his reception of Christ, seals him, by His indwelling presence, as the possession of Christ for ever (John 16:7-15; Eph. 1:13-14, 4:30; 1 Cor. 6:19-20).

(7) The eternal retribution of the wrath of God upon all who die unrepentant, either rejecting, neglecting or despising the salvation provided by the Son of God (John 3:36, 12:47-48; Mark 9:43-48; Rev. 20:11-15).

These are some of the fundamental truths of Christianity. It is written: "If the foundations be destroyed, what shall the righteous do?" (Ps. 11:3). Any person, calling himself a Christian, who flatly denies any of these truths is not a Christian at all, and therefore should not have any place in a company of sound believers at the Lord's supper. If such a person, who has "unawares crept in," is discovered, he should be examined by the elder brethren. If he is guilty of denying these truths, and refuses to repent, that person should be removed from that assembly. It may be, of course, that the person is ignorant of what the Word of God really teaches. In such a case, he should be instructed, and shown his error by a judicious use of the Scriptures by those who are well taught in the Word. These elder brethren are described as being "apt to teach, patient, in meekness instructing those who oppose themselves; if God peradventure will give them repentance to the acknowledging of the truth: and that they may recover themselves out of the snare of the Devil" (2 Tim. 2:24-26).

The Participants Should be Morally Clean

It is possible to be quite orthodox in doctrine and, at the same time, immoral in life. Many a professing Christian, whose head is in the clouds of ecclesiastical orthodoxy has his feet in the mire of questionable practices. Scripture makes clear that cleanliness of life is a necessary condition for worthy participation in the Lord's supper. In fact, we are definitely told: "If any man that is called a brother be a fornicator, or covetous, or a railer, or a drunkard, or an extortioner, with such an one, no not to eat" (1 Cor. 5:11). In the assembly at Corinth there was a man who had been guilty of gross immorality, and the believers were instructed to "Put away from among yourselves that wicked person" (1 Cor. 5:1-5, 13).

It is tragically possible for a person's life to give lie to his lips. It is one thing to *believe* the gospel, and another to "*behave* as becometh the gospel"

(Phil. 1:27). Bunyan speaks of a man named Talkative, who was "a saint abroad and a demon at home." Of a certain man it was said, "He preaches cream, but lives skimmed milk!" It is not an unknown combination for ecclesiastical rigidity to be accompanied by moral laxity, verbal chicanery, business dishonesty and religious hypocrisy.

What shame and disgrace has been brought to a company of Christians because of the inconsistent life of one who is associated with it! The Christian pathway is littered with those who have made moral wrecks of themselves. They once ran well, but began to neglect the cultivation of their spiritual life by Bible study and prayer. Soon they began to flirt with the world and pander to the lusts of the flesh, and by allowing their passions to get the better of them, fell into open sin which brought moral disaster to themselves, and disgrace to the assembly.

Paul realized this danger as to his own personal life, and consequently ruled himself with an iron hand. Notice what he says in this regard: "I keep under my body, and bring it into subjection: lest that by any means, when I have preached to others, I myself should be a castaway" (or set aside as unworthy of His service), 1 Corinthians 9:27. He was determined that his body should not be allowed to run away with him, but that he should always be in control of it. This is the price we must pay for usefulness in the Lord's service.

Where known moral evil in a believer's life is allowed to remain unjudged in a company of Christians, there will be a noticeable decline in the spiritual power of that assembly. This will be seen in a dearth of blessing, and a coldness of heart, together with a lack of love on the part of the believers. This moral evil, therefore, must be dealt with, painful though it is, and suitable discipline administered to the offender. Only in this way can the honor of the testimony be maintained.

When any believer is known, on the unimpeachable evidence of two or more witnesses, to be guilty of any of the sins ennumerated in 1 Corinthians 5:11, it is the solemn duty of the elder brethren to approach such a person, together with the witnesses, and deal faithfully with him in the matter. Likewise, any professing Christian, who seeks the fellowship of a company of believers, should have a clean bill of moral health, as well as being doctrinally sound. It is written: "Holiness becometh Thine house, O Lord, for ever" (Ps. 93:5).

It should be pointed out, however, that excommunication from an assembly is a *last resort*, and should be entered upon with extreme reluctance, and always with a view to the restoration of the offender. It is to be feared that some assemblies, to coin an expression, seem to be "excommunication happy." This, to them, is the panacea for every ill that may arise. It reminds one of the famous White Queen, in "Alice in Wonderland," whose favorite expression, when she heard of the delinquency of anyone was: "Off with his head!" There are many shades and grades of discipline described in the New Testament. To administer this discipline rightly calls for spiritual discernment of a high order. Where this is lacking, the guillotine is kept busy, with dire results. It is not written in vain: "If ye bite and devour one another, take heed that ye be not consumed one of another" (Gal. 5:15). Some assemblies have been known to excommunicate themselves out of existence!

Chapter Twelve

The Participants of the Lord's Supper:
Welcoming

Some scriptural principles governing the welcoming of believers to the Lord's Supper

Properly speaking, an assembly does not "*receive*" a fellow believer to the Lord's supper, but rather *welcomes* him. Let us illustrate this distinction in terms. Let us suppose that a person is a guest of the President at the White House. While he is there, the President decides to have a banquet and invites quite a number of people. When the guests respond to the invitation and arrive at the White House, who receives them, the guest or the host? There is only one answer to this question. You reply, and rightly, the President does the *receiving*. What, then, does the guest do? The guest simply *welcomes* his fellow guests who have responded to the invitation of the President. Now apply this to the Lord's supper. Who invites the guests? The Lord. Who receives the guests? The Lord. What do the believers do? They welcome their fellow guests who have responded to the invitation of their common Lord.

Now let us pursue the illustration a little further. Would this guest of the President, without consulting his host, take it upon himself to invite a number of his friends to the White House for supper? Of course not. This is the prerogative of the host alone. Likewise, Christians do not have any authority to invite people to the Lord's supper. They have the privilege of showing their fellow believers, from the Word, that the Lord has invited all His own, who are sound in life and doctrine, to His supper; but the accepting of and the responding to that invitation is the responsibility of each believer.

When a believer, sound in life and doctrine, presents himself at an assembly, and desires to remember the Lord in the breaking of bread, he should be welcomed by his fellow guests at the "feast of love Divine." Much heartache would have been avoided if this simple fact had been kept in mind. By adopting a harsh, rigid and exclusive attitude to their fellow believers, some assemblies have acted as though *they* were the *hosts* at the

Lord's supper, and consequently many true believers have been refused participation and thus denied their birthright privilege.

In this matter of welcoming believers to the Lord's supper, there are two extremes to be avoided: the extreme of ultra exclusivism on one hand, and the extreme of gross carelessness on the other. In the former case, some assemblies would impose, on the believer, other conditions than what the Word warrants, namely that the person is saved, is doctrinally sound and morally clean. They would insist that he agree to abide by certain of their own rules and regulations which are not laid down in the Word of God, ere he can be permitted to remember the Lord with them. In the case of the careless assembly, little or no care is exercised in welcoming one who desires to partake of the Lord's supper. The great necessity, therefore, is to firmly avoid both extremes.

Our Lord laid down a principle to which all assemblies should give good heed: "He that receiveth you, receiveth Me, and he that receiveth Me receiveth Him that sent Me" (Matt. 10:40). If the Lord has received a person, then what shall be said of that company that refuses to welcome him? In effect, it claims to be more particular and discriminating than the Lord Himself!

What mischief, and worse, has been wrought by a narrow, bigoted and tightlaced attitude adopted towards the Lord's people who do not see exactly as they do, but who love the Lord with as much devotion, and perhaps more, than they. Hundreds of simple believers have been stumbled by the harsh, uncharitable, censorious and ultra critical attitude and treatment adopted towards them by those who claimed to be "the-Lord's-gathered-out-people," as distinct from those contemptuously referred to as belonging to "the sects and the systems." If only such assemblies were as much interested in gathering *in* as they are in gathering *out*, there would be a revival among the dead bones!

Let us be clear on this matter of sectarianism. Any company of believers who claim to possess certain exclusive spiritual blessings that are not common to all other believers; or who designate themselves by a distinguishing name that is not common to all other believers; or who claim to have a superior status, in the sight of God, that is not true of other Christians; or who claim to have an exclusive monopoly of the presence of Christ in their midst, as distinct from other companies of believers, *is on sectarian ground.* Of all the sects of Christendom, the sect that claims to be unsectarian, but acts in a sectarian manner, is the worst sect of them all! It is possible to be most careful in the matter of breaking bread, and most callous in the matter of breaking hearts.

There is always the danger of going "beyond the things that are written" (2 Cor. 4:6 RV), and imposing conditions upon the welcoming of believers that the New Testament does not lay down. It is still possible for the traditions of men to supersede the authority of the Word of God (Matt. 15:9). It is sad to see an assembly more interested in ways and means of keeping Christians *out* than in thinking of ways and means of bringing them *in*. Any company of believers, that knowingly refuses to allow a believer, sound in doctrine and life, a place at the Lord's supper, constitutes itself, by that very act, a sect, however strenuously those composing it may deny the fact.

While ever maintaining godly care in welcoming Christians, let us keep an open heart for all the Lord's people, and show them that love, courtesy and consideration that is the evidence of real and vital Christianity. The words of our Lord should ever be kept in mind: "By this shall all men know that ye are My disciples, if ye have love one to another" (John 13:35).

In this connection, the weighty words of C. H. Mackintosh, author of the much used *Notes on the Penteteuch*, are worthy of our most serious consideration: "If there be any term of communion proposed, save the all important one of faith in the atonement of Christ and a walk consistent with that faith, the table ceases to be the Lord's, and becomes the table of a sect."

There are two ways of determining who shall, or who shall not be welcomed to the Lord's supper. One is to draw up a list of inflexible rules and regulations, either written or oral, to which every applicant must wholeheartedly agree ere he can enter their exclusive circle of fellowship. This, of course, answers to the book of discipline that is used in many denominations. This obviates the necessity for any real spiritual discernment, and becomes a purely mechanical process by which a certain uniformity of procedure is attained.

The other method is for each applicant to be considered on his own merits. This will involve the application of certain scriptural principles laid down in the Word of God, and applied by spiritual brethren, who are sensible, well taught in the Word, well balanced, gracious and considerate. These will interview the person who desires to break bread, and decide whether or not he should be welcomed. Happy is that assembly that has a number of such sound, spiritual and sensible men!

Perhaps some may be wondering what are the scriptural principles that should govern our judgment in these decisions.Let us look at some of them.

In the first place, a believer could be welcomed on his profession of faith in Christ. Through the hearing of the gospel, this person has come to realize his need as a lost sinner, and has believed the message of salvation through faith in the One who bore his sins and died to secure his deliverance. Upon accepting Christ and confessing Him as Lord, he has been baptized, and now desires to observe the Lord's supper. Such a person, of course, is warmly welcomed, as a known believer.

Again, a person may be vouched for by a brother or sister in whom the assembly has confidence. This is illustrated in the case of the apostle Paul. On his return from Damascus, where he had been saved, he attempted to meet with the believers in Jerusalem. Knowing that, at one time, Paul had been a bitter persecutor of Christians, the brethren were afraid to welcome him. Barnabas, however, a brother in whom they had every confidence, recommended him to the assembly and, on his testimony, Paul was allowed to come among them (Acts 9:19-29).

Then again, the person who comes to the assembly may carry a letter of commendation which his home assembly has given him. This letter, signed by the responsible brethren, commends this person to the love and care of any company of believers meeting on scriptural lines. On the strength of this letter, the believer is welcomed (2 Cor. 3:1-4).

We must beware, however, of allowing this form of procedure to become a fixed and inflexible rule governing the welcoming of believers. It has happened too often that a carnal believer, who carries a letter of commendation from his home assembly, has been welcomed to the breaking of bread; while a deeply spiritual believer, who does not carry such a letter, is refused the privilege of partaking of the Lord's supper. Thus one person's ecclesiastical *connection* is given preference to another's spiritual *character*, and this is definitely not of God. Spiritual character must always be preferred to ecclesiastical connection.

Once more, a well known and respected preacher, or teacher of the Word, will not need any letter of commendation. His work has already commended him to the attention of the Lord's people. However, if such a person were to go to another country, where he is not known, it certainly would be advisable for him to take a letter of commendation with him. Paul came under this classification and wrote: "Need we, as some others. epistles of commendation to you or from you?" (2 Cor. 3:1).

There are cases, however that do not come under any of these categories. Here is a godly person, sound in doctrine and life, but who has been identified with a denomination for many years. This person has been brought to see, by his study of the Word of God, the unscripturalness of his position. He has been led to realize that denominationalism and clerisy have no support in the New Testament. Accordingly, he presents himself at an assembly of believers and desires to meet with them. What is to be done in this case? He should be interviewed by a few courteous, well taught, and spiritually discerning brethren. With judicious questioning, they can soon determine if he is a real child of God and thus qualified to remember the Lord in the breaking of bread.

However, there may be some things that this brother has not yet seen, due to his long association with the denomination he has just left. For instance, he may not be clear on the subject of believer's baptism by immersion, subsequent to conversion. By all means let this matter be placed before him in a kindly and faithful manner, but it should not be made the *condition* on which he is allowed to take the Lord's supper. To force his submission to a rite that he *cannot see*, in order to enable him to comply with an ordinance that he *can see*, is not only to go beyond the Word of God, but is the height of unreasonableness.

We must ever keep in mind that we are living in the midst of something that the New Testament does not directly contemplate, namely, a baptized mass of humanity. Practically every genuine Christian we meet has passed through some form of baptism, so called. In a great number of cases he was sprinkled with water as a baby. When, in later years, he was saved by the grace of God, he was given to understand that this christening was the equivalent of believer's baptism, and his denomination encouraged him in this belief.

We should not expect this Christian to see, in an hour, what it has taken us years to learn! Let us encourage him to act upon what he *does* see. As he does so, God will give him more light on what he cannot see now, for it is written: "For with Thee is the fountain of life. In Thy light we shall see light" (Ps. 36:9). In any case, as we have found out for ourselves, it is much harder to unlearn than to learn! As this person comes under the ministry of the Word, in the congenial atmosphere of a spiritual assembly, marked by a love for all the saints, he will develop in his understanding of the truth, and "grow in grace and in the knowledge of the Lord."

Apollos is a case in point. He is described as being "an eloquent man and mighty in the Scriptures," but he was not clear on the question of baptism. Fortunately, there was a godly couple, Aquila and Priscilla, in whose home the assembly met. They took him aside, "and expounded unto him the way of God more perfectly" (Acts 18:24-28; 1 Cor. 16:19).

Let us beware of *spiritual* snobbery, which causes believers to look down upon their fellow believers who do not have the amount of light on the Scriptures that they may have. Let us not make *light* on the Scriptures the test of fellowship, but *life* in Christ. There is no aristocracy in the family of God! All the members of that family have the same Father, the same Savior, the same indwelling Comforter, the same Bible, the same salvation, the same hope, the same blessings and the same eternal home. Of all Christians it is written: "Ye are all one in Christ Jesus" (Gal. 3:28). An old Christian used to say: "Keep the door of the gospel open for all sinners, and the door of the assembly open for all saints."

An assembly must also beware of *social* snobbery, and the forming of cliques. James condemns this in unsparing fashion. Mark well his words: "My brethren, have not the faith of our Lord Jesus Christ, the Lord of glory, with respect of persons. For if there come into your assembly a man with a gold ring, in goodly apparel, and there come in also a poor man in vile raiment; and ye have respect to him that weareth the gay clothing, and say unto him: 'Sit thou here in a good place'; and say to the poor, 'Stand thou there, or sit here under my footstool'; are ye not then partial in yourselves, and are become judges of evil thoughts? . . . If ye have respect to persons, ye commit sin and are convinced of the laws as transgressors" (James 2:1-9).

There can be no class distinctions at the Lord's supper. All believers occupy one common position as "priests unto God." The fact that one Christian has more money, or a better job, or lives in a better house than another, does not elevate him to a higher plane in God's sight. We are exhorted to "Mind not high things, but condescend to (or go along with) men of low estate. Be not wise in your own conceits" (Rom. 12:16).

Sometimes it happens that Christians from some denomination will come to the Lord's supper, not to break bread, but simply to observe what takes place at such a meeting. They are not clear in their own minds as to what the New Testament teaches in this regard, but are willing to learn. What a privilege it is to meet such, and to help them on their way! These should also be contacted in their homes and dealt with wisely. Each assembly would be well advised to have some good literature on hand to give to such. Many have been led to see these scriptural principles of gathering as a result of a careful reading of such literature in the light of the Word of God.

We could not conclude this rather long section better than by referring the reader to John Bunyan's immortal allegory, *The Pilgrim's Progress*. The pilgrim is described as coming to the Castle Beautiful, which, of course, pictures a scripturally gathered company of believers. At the door he was met by a woman named Discretion, who questioned him as to his profession of faith in Christ and his manner of life. Once she was satisfied as to the reality of his experience of the saving grace of God, she passed him on to her three sisters, whose names were Prudence, Piety and Charity, who engaged him in further conversation.

These four sisters represent four virtues, or graces, that should characterize every company of believers. First, there should be *discretion* in welcoming a person who desires to meet with an assembly. Second, there should be *prudence*, or sound common sense. Third, there should be *piety*, or godliness. Last, but by no means least, there should be *charity*, or love. As these four virtues are allowed to have full and harmonious expression in a company of believers, the saints will be edified, and God will add others of His people to that assembly because, in such an atmosphere, they will be led on in ways pleasing to Himself.

We have spent considerable time on this matter of welcoming our fellow believers. We have done so deliberately, because it is a matter of controversy in some quarters, where rigid views are looked upon as being "scriptural," and true to what they call: the "old paths." Let us seek to hold and maintain a proper balance in regard to these things, and make the principles of Scripture our sole guide in this matter.

Chapter Thirteen

The Procedure of the Lord's Supper:
Place, Requirements

By this we mean the manner in which the Lord's supper was observed, as recorded in the New Testament.

As to the Place

The New Testament has nothing to say about "consecrated places of worship." There is no mention of imposing cathedrals, chapels, or even "gospel halls!" From the Old Testament scriptures we learn that the Tabernacle was the dwelling place of God (Ex. 25:8; Num. 5:2-3). Later on, a Temple was erected in Jerusalem and it, too, was sanctified by the shekinah glory of God (1 Kings 8:10-11; 2 Chron. 5:13-14). Both the Tabernacle and the Temple were called "the house of God" (Judg. 18:31; 2 Chron. 22:12).

At the death of Christ, the veil that separated the holy place from the holy of holies was rent in twain from top to bottom, in the midst. This was intended by God to indicate that the Aaronic priesthood, together with the temple and all the elaborate ritual and its many sacrifices, had been brought to an end. Thus an entirely new dispensation was introduced in which God was now prepared to receive, pardon, welcome, justify and relieve the vilest sinner who would rest in the eternal efficacy of the once-for-all substitutionary sacrifice of the Son of God, trust Him as Savior, and own Him as Lord.

In the early days of Christianity, the Temple still continued to function. The rent veil was mended, and the priests went through all the usual motions, offered the same sacrifices with the same elaborate ritual; but the whole thing was utterly valueless in the sight of God. Hebrews 10:11 sums it up thus: "And every priest standeth daily ministering and offering oftentimes the same sacrifices which can *never take away sins.*" In AD 70, Titus, the Roman emperor, beseiged the city of Jerusalem, destroyed the temple, and thus brought to an end, *physically* and materially, what Christ had terminated *spiritually* by His death and resurrection many years before.

In fact, the Lord had prophesied the destruction of the temple, and told exactly how it was going to take place. (See Luke 19:41-44.)

God no longer dwells "in temples made by hands" (Acts 17:24-28). No material building, erected by man, can be described as "the house of God." The word, "church," in the New Testament, *never refers to a material building of wood, stone or brick*. The word is "ecclesia," which means, "assembly." It is so translated three times in Acts 19:32, 39, 41. The word "church," in its local aspect, simply refers to a number of Christians, in a certain area, who assemble together, in the name of the Lord Jesus, to remember Him in the breaking of bread, or for worship, praise, prayer or the ministry of the Word of God. Thus it is the *people*, and not the *building* in which they meet, that constitutes the church.

In the early days of Christianity, many of these assemblies met together in private homes, hence the expression: "The church that is in his house." (See Rom. 16:5; 1 Cor. 16:19; Philem. 2.) In those days, there were no huge buildings, such as cathedrals, which are now viewed as being sacrosanct by virtue of an elaborate ceremony of "consecration." The truth is that a building is not even necessary for the observance of the Lord's supper. It can be held in the open air, in a tent, or a soldier's barrack room, where a few Christian soldiers have come together to remember the Lord. The place where it is observed is therefore entirely immaterial. The Lord's supper can be observed *anywhere*.

It is not suggested, of course, that any old ramshackle building is good enough in which to meet, if some more suitable building can be obtained. Many assemblies today own their own buildings, not only for the purpose of breaking bread, but for other meetings, such as the preaching of the gospel to the unsaved, the conducting of a Sunday school, and the ministry of the Word, etc. Such a building, of course, should meet certain requirements of decency and fitness, which should enable both young and old to hear the Word of God in some degree of comfort.

There are some who would have us believe that the Lord's supper is *exclusively* a "church act." They affirm that unless there is a regularly constituted and "recognized" church, with its complement of proper gift in the way of evangelists, pastors and teachers, the Lord's supper cannot be observed! To this we reply that the New Testament, our sole authority on all such matters, says nothing of the kind! It is to be feared that those who teach this are more concerned about a *mode of procedure* than the value and the purpose of the simple memorial.

This idea, if accepted, would rob the Lord's supper of its beautiful simplicity. It would deny to a group of Christian soldiers, in some far off battlefield, the privilege of coming together to remember the Lord in the way He appointed. It would prohibit a small group of pioneer missionaries the right to assemble on a Lord's day to break bread. It would prevent a number of Christians, who, for some reason, find themselves on a Lord's day far removed from an assembly, from meeting in the name of their Lord to do what He requested. It would refuse to allow one or two of the brethren to go to the home of some aged or infirm saint, who was unable to go to the meeting place, and give him the privilege of taking the bread and the cup.

It would impose an embargo on the observance of the Lord's supper at a Summer Bible Conference, where a group of believers have gathered together to enjoy the ministry of the word of God for a few weeks. It was of such a conference that the remark was made: "I could not go there to break bread because they have moved the Lord's table from ___________ to ___________!" It would deny to Christians, travelling by sea, the privilege of meeting together "in the Savior's name, and breaking bread at His command." A well known teacher once remarked: "It is possible for Christians, when they wish to appear to be most solemn, to be, in reality, most silly!"

It certainly was not a "church act," when it was first instituted by the Lord Jesus, for the church was not then in existence! Nor was it a "church act" when it was celebrated *daily* in the homes of the early believers. (See Acts 2:46.) The word used for eating their meat is different from the one used to describe their breaking of bread. To those who say that v. 46 only describes the regular eating of their daily meals, we reply it seems hardly necessary to call particular attention to this fact, for Christians usually continue to eat their regular meals after they are saved! It is their "breaking bread at home," (marg.) to which our attention is called in this passage. As time went on, this ceased to be a daily thing and, by the period described in Acts 20:7, it had become a weekly observance.

Sometime ago, an article appeared in a magazine, in which the writer labored hard to attempt to prove that there must have been an assembly in the town of Troas, otherwise Paul and his companions would not have been able to break bread on that first day of the week! It all goes to prove that when a person formulates a theory, he will stop at nothing to attempt to support it from Scripture.

There are always those whose great ambition seems to be to set up a rigid code of laws, complete with a host of bylaws by which to govern a circle of assemblies of the Lord's people. They appear to be constituted in "the *objective* case and the *kickative* mood." They seem to be always looking for a place to build a *wall* where God has placed a *gate*! We must view these attempts to encroach on our liberty in Christ in the same way that Paul did to those in his day, who would have added restrictions to "the simplicity that is in Chrst Jesus." He declared emphatically: "To whom we gave place by subjection, no; not for an hour!" (Gal. 2:5). It is quite true that believers *normally* meet together, in assembly fellowship, to partake of the Lord's supper, and thus it becomes part of their church life; but to *limit* its observance to these occasions is to be "wise above that which is written."

A common expression, used by those who hold these rigid views, is that when a few believers meet together to remember the Lord Jesus they have "set up the Lord's table." As we have seen earlier, no one can "set up the Lord's table," for it has been set up by the Lord for many hundreds of years, and all believers are viewed by God as already at it from the moment of their conversion.

We must stedfastly refuse to allow any man, or group of men, however gifted and sincere in his purpose, to draw up a list of rules and regulations the Bible knows nothing about, by which to govern the policy of a certain group of assemblies. We must also constantly beware of allowing a custom, often repeated, to develop into a tradition which, in turn, comes to be looked upon as being "scriptural." It is interesting to see that, even under the law, there was an exception made with those Israelites who could not keep the Passover in the first month, and they were allowed, by God, to keep it in the second month (Num. 9:1-12).

Someone has pointed out that most religious movements usually have four stages. It begins with a *man*, who sees a certain truth. It is made known by a *message*. This, in turn, develops into a *movement*, which gradually loses its power and degenerates into a *monument*. As such, it ceases to be of any present vital force. No movement is immune from this danger. To be forewarned is to be forearmed. The Lord deliver us from becoming a dead monument to truth; but may we ever be a living testimony to the all sufficiency of the Word of God as the only foundation for faith and practice. May those assemblies of believers, who seek to meet on scriptural lines, be ever marked by spiritual freshness, sound teaching, earnest devotion to Christ and warm Christian love to all the saints!

As to the Requirements

Again it is simplicity itself. All that is needed is a loaf of bread and a cup containing the fruit of the vine. The kind of bread and wine, as we have already seen, is entirely immaterial. Though a table on which to place the elements is useful, it is not essential. Seats are handy things to have, but in the open air, even these would not be necessary. The table on which the elements are placed must not be thought of as "the Lord's table," in the sense of 1 Corinthians 10, but simply viewed as a useful piece of furniture. As to the arrangement of the chairs, whether they are to form a circle around the table, or face in one direction, we are not told. There does not have to be a circle to ensure that Christ may be "in the midst," for He has promised to be in the midst of "two or three," and these could hardly form a circle. Whatever arrangement is best suited to the meeting place would therefore be in order.

Perhaps some may be wondering: But what about the "officiating clergyman" who must be there to dispense the elements? The answer is: there is no such person mentioned in the New Testament. In many denominations today there could be no observance of the Lord's supper apart from the presence of an "ordained clergyman." Thus it would appear that it is not so much the presence of the Lord in the midst of His people that gives the Lord's supper its authority and value, but the presence of a person the Bible knows nothing about! In many cases this clergyman may not be saved by the grace of God, and consequently is incapable of either understanding or expounding spiritual realities.

We turn, therefore, with abhorrence from the proud pretentions of clerisy, with its distinctive dress, its claim to a superior status among Christians, its assumption of titles descriptive only of Deity such as: "reverend," "right reverend," "very reverend," "most reverend," and so on, right up to "holy father." The Bible knows nothing of this special caste among Christians.

Perhaps the question may be asked: "Who, then, should break the bread and pass the cup after the giving of thanks?" Again the answer is simple. Either the one who has given thanks for it or some other brother. In any case, the person who breaks the bread is only acting on behalf of the whole assembly. He does it merely as a convenience, so that it may be distributed more easily to all who are present. In fact, the person who breaks the bread on behalf of the whole assembly, also breaks it for himself when it is passed to him. The same is also true of the cup. This act does not give this person a superior status, or turn him into an "officiating priest." He is not taking the place of the Lord Jesus, but simply performing a useful service on behalf of his fellow believers.

Neither is there anything said as to whether the same person who gives thanks for the bread should also give thanks for the cup. In some assemblies this is looked upon as being "scriptural," for did not the Lord give thanks for both? This is true, but the one who gives thanks for the bread is not taking the place of the Lord Jesus, neither he that gives thanks for the cup. There is no rule, in the New Testament, in regard to this matter.

It all goes to show that an act, if repeated often enough, becomes a habit. This habit, in turn, hardens into a custom. This, through the years, develops into a tradition. Finally, after the passage of years, it comes to be looked upon as being "scriptural," whereas it has no scriptural authority whatever to back it up.

Some years ago, at a Bible conference, a brother remarked: "It was too bad to see the confusion at the Lord's supper this morning." Another brother replied: "Confusion? I didn't see any confusion. What was it?" The brother answered: "Didn't you notice that a different person gave thanks for the cup than gave thanks for the bread?" The other replied: "Why, that is not confusion! I've been accustomed to that mode of procedure ever since I began to break bread thirty years ago!" Thus, what was "confusion" to one, was "order" to the other! There is not even the mention of an elder or teacher in connection with the Lord's supper.

Needless to say, there is also no mention of an "altar," or a roped off "sanctuary" for the clergy. No mention also of a prayer book, or a prescribed order of service. All these things have been introduced by man, and undoubtedly have an appeal to the flesh, but they have no scriptural authority whatever. They have been borrowed from both Judaism and Paganism. The result is a mixture far removed from the pattern that God has given for His people in His Word.

Chapter Fourteen

The Procedure of the Lord's Supper:
Order: Guidance, Expression, Praise and Worship

As to the Order Observed

As far as we can see, there was only one *regular* meeting for Christians described in the New Testament, and this is the Lord's supper. The first reference to it is in Acts 2:42, where we are told that those saved on the day of Pentecost were baptized and "continued steadfastly (not spasmodically) in the apostles' doctrine, and fellowship and breaking of bread and prayers." In Acts 20:7, there is described what had then become the weekly custom of the early Church: "Upon the first day of the week when the disciples came together to break bread."

First Corinthians 11:23-34 contains the Lord's own revelation to Paul concerning this ordinance. Note particularly vs. 18 and 20 where we read, "When ye come together in the church," and, "When ye come together therefore into one place." Now compare these expressions with what is found in 1 Corinthians 14:23, 26, where we read, "If therefore the whole church be come together," and, "When ye come together." Thus both these passages refer to a coming together, and the purpose of this coming together was to remember the Lord in the breaking of bread. From 1 Corinthians 14:16 we gather that the "giving of thanks" refers to the Lord's supper, and that edifying ministry of the Word followed the breaking of bread.

While no set rules of procedure are laid down for the Lord's supper, yet certain broad principles are indicated for our guidance in this matter, and these are viewed as being authoritative, for we read: "If any man thinketh himself to be a prophet or spiritual, let him acknowledge that the things which I write unto you are the commandments of the Lord" (1 Cor. 14:27). We shall do well, therefore, to give good heed to these principles, for they have the highest authority for their observance. We shall consider seven of these principles.

1. The principle of divine guidance

Inasmuch as there is no mention of any definite mode of procedure, or program for the observance of the Lord's supper, it is obvious that the Lord Himself is viewed as being in the midst of His gathered people, as the Host to preside. This is in fulfilment of His own promise: "For where two or three are gathered together in My name, there am I in the midst of them" (Matt. 18:20). Christ is there, as both the Head of the Church and the Host at His own supper. He was the Host at its first institution, and He has not resigned, or delegated anyone else to take His place! The Christians who are present are not only members of His body, but also His very highly privileged and greatly honored guests.

Surely nothing could be more desirable to the believer than this! Thus there is to be no one at this supper to take His place, and rob Him of the preeminence that is His due. It is *His* supper, and the saints are there to honor Him. Who then would dare to attempt to take His place and arrange its program?

But more, the Holy Spirit indwells each Christian, and it is His delight to so impress the hearts of the believers with the excellences, glories, beauties and perfection of the Lord Jesus that there shall rise, from their redeemed spirits, such praise, worship and adoration as shall bring delight to the One who alone is worthy. When the blessed Holy Spirit is allowed to remain ungrieved by any misconduct on the part of the believer, and unquenched by any disobedience to His leading, such a meeting will be the nearest thing to heaven on earth for those who are there.

As the Lord's people come together, with prepared hearts, to remember Him, they can truthfully sing:

> With Jesus in our midst,
> We gather round the board;
> Though many, we are one in Christ,
> One body in the Lord.
>
> (R. C. Chapman)

Some years ago, at a large conference, one of the speakers invited a lawyer friend to come to the meeting for the breaking of bread, observe what took place, and report to him afterwards his impressions of the meeting. Accordingly this friend, who was an unsaved man, took his seat in the gallery and watched over one thousand people take their place around a table on which was a large loaf of bread and many cups of wine. The meeting continued for over an hour in perfect harmony. He saw one brother after another rise, either to give out a hymn, or lead the assembly in worship. Then thanks was given for the bread and it was broken and passed around. Then thanks was given for the cup, and it was passed from lip to lip.

At the conclusion of the meeting his friend asked him: "Well, what did you think of that meeting?" The lawyer replied: "Well, I don't know who arranged that service, but whoever he was, he certainly knew his business!" Yes, the Holy Spirit knows His business, and this is never more clearly demonstrated than at a meeting for the remembrance of the Lord Jesus, when He is allowed to preside and guide.

2. The principle of liberty of expression

One has only to read 1 Corinthians 14 to be impressed with the fact that there was no such thing as a "one-man-ministry" in those days. Neither will he receive the impression that it was an "any-man-ministry," for only those brethren who were divinely fitted and guided were to take part. Thus, while there was perfect freedom for the brethren to give vocal expression to their thoughts, there was to be no license, or a do-as-you-please attitude adopted on the part of the saints. We read: "All may prophecy, one by one, that all may learn and all may be comforted" (v. 31). Thus it was a "one-at-a-time" ministry.

He refers to the fact that "every one of you hath a psalm, hath a doctrine, hath a tongue, hath a revelation, hath an interpretation. Let all things be done unto edifying" (v. 26). Paul, by the Spirit, is not condemning this multiplicity of expression, but merely urging upon them the necessity for its proper regulation, so that there should be no confusion. The women are expressly commanded to be silent in the churches, for "it is not permitted unto them to speak" (v. 35). Thus we learn that vocal worship, and the ministry of the Word that followed, were not confined to one person.

All the believers present had been constituted "a kingdom of priests unto God," and were therefore at liberty to offer the sacrifice of praise, the brethren *audibly* and the sisters *inaudibly* (Rev. 1:5; 5:10; 1 Peter 2:5-10). Therefore, to limit the audible expression of prayer, praise, worship and the ministry of the Word to *one person*, at such a meeting, is to go contrary to the principles found in the New Testament.

Christendom has done this, with disastrous results. In altogether too many places the "officiating clergyman" has never been born again, and consequently is unable either to perceive, much less to impart divine truth to the members of his congregation. In the case where the minister is a saved person, the ministry of the Word is necessarily limited in its expression to this one individual. He must therefore be the sole preacher, teacher, evangelist and pastor, but seldom are all these gifts found in one person. God's Word puts it thus: "And He gave some apostles; and some, prophets; and some, evangelists; and some, pastors and teachers; for the perfecting of the saints, for the work of the ministry, for the edifying of the body of Christ" (Eph. 4:11-12).

Thus there should be a *multiplicity* of gift in an assembly of the Lord's people. In the assembly at Philippi there were many "bishops and deacons." See Phil. 1:2. The remedy for any confusion that might possibly arise from this liberty of oral expression is not to substitute a one-man-ministry for it; but for the brethren to humbly submit to the guidance of the Word of God in the matter of its proper regulation in the assembly. We cannot improve on the pattern given to us in the Word, for this is our sole guide.

3. The principle of praise and worship

At this meeting of the believers, praise and worship formed no small part, for they had come primarily to remember the Lord, and to give Him thanks for all that He was, and for all He had done. Thus we read of "the giving of thanks" (1 Cor. 11:24; 14:16).

As early as around AD 110, Pliny, governor of Bithynia, at the request of the Roman emperor Trajan, investigated the doings of the people called Christians. He reported as follows: "The whole crime, or the error of the Christians, lay in this: they were accustomed, on a certain day, to meet before daylight, and to sing among themselves a hymn to Christ as God, and to bind themselves by an oath not to commit any wickedness, nor to be guilty of theft, or robbery, or adultery; never to falsify their word, nor to deny a pledge committed to them when called upon to return it." Thus does a secular historian record the purpose for which these early assemblies came together on "a certain day"; the Lord's day, of course.

Praise and worship, though characteristic of the Lord's supper, should most certainly not be *confined* to this meeting. Praise and worship is essentially an *individual* thing which should be true of the Christian wherever he is, each day of the week. It is not something to be stored up and reserved until the weekly remembrance at the Lord's supper. There is not much likelihood of praise and worship at this meeting if the saints have not been praiseful and worshipful during the week.

John could say: "I was in the Spirit on the Lord's day" (Rev. 1:10). The reason for this was that he had been in the Spirit on the previous six days of the week! Some Christians have the peculiar notion that they can live carnal lives from Monday to Saturday and expect, in some mysterious and magical fashion, to wake up on Sunday morning and find themselves "in the Spirit"! Nothing could be further from the truth.

The spiritual atmosphere of a gathering of believers will be determined by the spirituality of each one present, sisters as well as brethren. An assembly is made up of individuals, and the spiritual quality of the whole is determined by the spiritual quality of each part. A good question for each Christian to put to himself is: "What contribution am I making to the spiritual tone of the assembly of which I form a part?"

There is no meeting on earth that is so calculated to lift the believer to a high spiritual plane, than a Spirit-led and Spirit-empowered meeting for the remembrance of the Lord Jesus. From the assembled believers, there rises a volume of praise and worship, as one after another voices his appreciation of the One in whose name they have met. As they thus concentrate on the Person and work of their blessed Lord, and give Him the place of preeminence, as the Lord in their midst, hearts are bowed with wonder and worship. Nothing can take the place of this meeting. It is unique in Christendom. May it be ours to value it more and more, and so live that we shall be in the position and condition to worship Him in Spirit and in truth! (John 4:24).

4. The principle of edifying ministry

While the celebration of the Lord's supper was the *principal* purpose for which the Christians came together, it was not the *only* purpose. Following the breaking of bread, there was a period devoted to the ministry of the Word by those whom the Lord had gifted, and who were so led by the Holy Spirit to do so. Two or three would rise to address the company and thus the assembly was edified.

The profitable regulation of this ministry is the subject of 1 Corinthians 14. These Corinthian believers were greatly gifted, particularly in speech. It appears that sometimes their zeal outran their sense of judgment. The result was a confusion of voices, and this definitely was not the godly order that should characterize such a gathering. Paul reminds them that "God is not the Author of confusion, but of peace, as in all the Churches of the saints" (v. 33).

It is therefore quite scriptural for an assembly, after the breaking of bread, to give one or more of the brethren the opportunity to minister the Word of God to the edification of those gathered. In fact, very often, this is the only opportunity some believers will have to hear an exposition from Scriptures for the rest of the week. This ministry, we are told, was to serve a threefold purpose, "edification, exhortation and comfort" (vs. 3, 6).

The word, "prophesy" (v. 1) does not necessarily mean *fore*telling of future events, but rather the *forth*telling of the mind of God. A prophet has been well described as: "One who is so in communion with God that he is able to communicate His mind." In the days in which Paul wrote, there was no New Testament, as we now have it. For practically twenty-five years, after the ascension of Christ, there were no New Testament writings. Probably the first to appear was the epistle of James, around AD 49. The first epistle to the Corinthians was written around AD 54 or 55. It is somewhat difficult to determine the exact date of the apperance of these various books which now combine to form the New Testament, as we have it at this present time.

In view of the fact that there was no completed Bible, Paul describes these believers in Corinth as coming to the assembly, each having either "a psalm," a "doctrine," a "tongue," a "revelation" and "an interpretation" (v. 26). Thus God, in a special and miraculous way, enabled these various brethren to communicate the mind of God according to the ability with which He had gifted them, and in the power of the Holy Spirit.

Today of course, we have the completed revelation of the mind of God in the divinely inspired Scriptures. There is therefore no need for tongues, or for prophecies, in the sense of foretelling. "When that which is perfect is come, then that which is in part shall be done away" (1 Cor. 13:8-10). By this we understand that the expression, "that which is perfect," refers to the completed Canon of Scripture, which has eliminated any further need for a special revelation to supplement the Word of God. Prophecy now consists of the explanation and application of the Word of God, which has already been recorded for our doctrine or teaching, "reproof, correction and instruction in righteousness" (2 Tim. 3:16). With this distinction in our minds, let us see what is involved by the term, "edifying ministry."

(a) It should follow the breaking of bread

The purpose of the Lord's supper, as we have seen, is to enable the believers present to concentrate their attention and affection on the Person of the Lord Jesus, and thus remember Him to the exclusion of all else. Since this is so, then it would logically follow that any ministry *before* the breaking of bread, which would tend to distract the attention of Christians from the Person of Christ, would not *properly belong* to this part of the meeting. Such ministry might be perfectly appropriate *after* the breaking of bread.

If this simple principle were laid to heart, by those who seek to minister the Word of God, there would be more worship addressed to the Father and the Son than exhortation addressed to the saints during this first part of the service. Any ministry, prior to the breaking of bread, should therefore be calculated to occupy the believers with the Lord Jesus, so that their hearts may be led out to further praise and worship.

It is wise, therefore, for an assembly to allow a period of time after the breaking of bread for any word of ministry which will be to the edification, exhortation and comfort of those gathered. It sometimes happens that the flow of worship, from the believers, has been interrupted by some brother, who took advantage of a pause to deliver a message which he mistakenly imagined the Lord had given him, but which contained no reference whatever to the Person of Christ, or the purpose for which the saints had come together. Surely, such things ought not so to be. It is possible for Christians to meet in a scriptural manner, in the name of the Lord Jesus, and for a scriptural purpose, the rememberance of Christ, and yet fall short in fulfilling that purpose because of unreasonable ministry. Brethren, "suffer the word of exhortation," for it is much needed.

Chapter Fifteen

The Procedure of the Lord's Supper:
Order: Edifying, Harmony and Order

(b) It should be intelligent

By this we mean that any ministry given should be spiritually informative, enlightening and appropriate to the needs of the people of God. He who speaks should, like Haggai, be "the Lord's messenger in the Lord's message" (Hag. 1:13). We have all been made to realize that it is possible for a person to say nothing at extreme length. God's word to Job is pertinent to this: "Who is this that darkeneth counsel by words without knowledge?" (Job 38:2).

Some open their mouths just in order to say something, but others because they have something to say. Herein lies the difference between unprofitable and profitable ministry. The ministry of the Word, given on such an occasion, may be the result of careful and prayerful preparation, or it may be spontaneous. In both cases, the speaker should be fully persuaded in his own mind that this is the message the Lord would have him to pass on to the assembly.

Such ministry may take the form of exhortation in order to stir up the saints to greater devotion to Christ. It may consist of rebuke, drawing their attention to some lack in their lives. It may be to comfort, encourage and cheer those who are passing through trial, persecution, loss or bereavement. It may be an exposition of some passage of Scripture that is calculated to build up the believers and establish them in the Word of God. Whatever form the ministry may take, it should be spiritual, sound and sensible.

Paul declared that he would rather speak five words with his understanding than ten thousand words which could not be understood. Again he exhorts them: "Brethren, be not children in understanding . . . but in understanding be men" (1 Cor. 14:19-20). God places no premium on ignorance, but desires His people to "have their senses exercised to discern both good and evil" (Heb. 5:14). God has given certain senses to His people, and not the least of these is common sense.

While it is perfectly true that all believers are priests unto God, yet it is equally true that not all believers have been gifted of God with the ability to publicly preach and teach the Word of God. This is one of the gifts of the risen Head to the members of His body, the Church. Paul, by the Spirit, urges believers first to earnestly desire these spiritual gifts and then, when received, to develop them by study and exercise; for gifts, through neglect and disuse, may be lost. Particularly does he emphasize the importance of the gift of prophecy, or the forthtelling of the Word of God (1 Cor. 14:1-3). Thus intelligent and edifying ministry plays no small part in the spiritual growth of an assembly, as the Christians gather to remember Him.

(c) It should be intelligible

However good the spoken ministry may be, if it is not distinctly heard, it will profit no one. Scripture puts it thus: "Else when thou shalt bless with the spirit, how shall he that occupieth the room of the unlearned say, "Amen," at thy giving of thanks, seeing he understandeth not what thou sayest? For verily thou givest thanks well, but the other is not edified" (1 Cor. 14:16-17). Who has not wilted under the ministry of a person who speaks in so low a tone, or so indistinctly, that no one could understand what he was talking about.

It seems obvious that a person who cannot make himself heard, or understood, should not rise to speak in an assembly, for he is only wasting the valuable time of those present. Public ministry is intended by God for the profit of all, and it cannot be profitable unless it is understood. Paul puts it thus: "So likewise ye, except ye utter by the tongue words easy to be understood, how shall it be known what is spoken? for ye shall speak into the air" (v. 9).

Sometimes this indistinctness of utterance is due to the fact that the speaker does not face the majority of his audience. Each speaker therefore should not only face his audience, but also suit the tone and volume of his voice to the size of the building and the number of his audience. Herein lies the value of the use of that "sound mind" that God has given to us (2 Tim. 1:7).

(d) It should be brief

A long prosy address only succeeds in defeating its purpose. The "five words," spoken with the understanding, are to be preferred to the long address. A brief, pithy, pertinent and pungent message will long linger in the memory of the hearers, while the noise of "words of learned length and thundering sound" will soon be forgotten. A brief address will also give an opportunity for someone else to speak who has a word from the Lord. Naturally, the speaker will be guided by the amount of time at his disposal, so that he will not inconvenience the saints by unduly prolonging his message. The speaker, if a visitor, would do well to inquire just when the meeting is supposed to end, and be guided accordingly in any ministry he gives from the Word.

(e) It should be with self restraint

When a speaker loses his self control and indulges in a wild harangue of words, it is evident the ministry is not to edification. The last mentioned quality of the "fruit of the Spirit" is temperance, or self control (Gal. 5:22-23). We are informed that "the spirit of the prophets are subject to the prophets" (v. 32). To have a mere impulse to speak is not an indication it is of the Lord. It may be of the flesh, and entirely inappropriate to the present occasion. Each speaker therefore should set a guard upon his lips, lest they are allowed to rob him of his poise, self possession and self control. The extravagances of the "tongues movement" will serve to illustrate what happens when people allow their minds to go blank, abandon all efforts at self control, and obey every impulse that comes into the mind. The result is disorder and this, we know from the Word, is *not of God*.

It is sometimes asserted, without any scriptural authority, that all ministry at the Lord's supper should be unpremeditated and spontaneous. Obviously, this is not so, for both are suggested in 1 Corinthians 14. Spontaneity is in view in verse 30; while premeditation, and its necessary preparation, is in view in verse 36. Therefore it is perfectly correct for a believer to carefully and prayerfully prepare a message, and go ready to give it should the Lord so lead, and the opportunity be provided.

However, he should not go *determined* to deliver it, whether it is suitable to the occasion or not. By all means, let the believer go prepared to give his message, but let him also be prepared *not* to give it. It often happens that a speaker realizes that the message he thought of giving would be inappropriate to this particular occasion, and consequently refrains from giving it, or perhaps gives an entirely different message from the one he thought of giving. As the believer walks in the fear of the Lord and the comfort of the Holy Spirit, he will become sensitive to the leading of the Spirit (Acts 9:31).

(f) It should be with consideration for others

We read: "If anything be revealed to another that sitteth by; let the first hold his peace, for ye may all prophesy one by one, that all may learn, and all may be comforted" (1 Cor. 14:30-31). The fact that a person thinks God has given him a message does not mean that he must either belittle or interrupt another speaker, for this is neither godly order nor Christian courtesy. It is quite possible for a believer to be sincerely mistaken in thinking he has a message from the Lord. Perhaps the other brother is the one who should give the message for this occasion. Far better then, that he should hold his peace until his brother is through with his message.

If God has really given a person a message, He will provide the opportunity for its delivery in His own good time and way. God is never in a hurry, and He has declared: "He that believeth shall not make haste" (Isa. 26:18). There is no need therefore for impatience. Perhaps another time would be much more suitable. Some addresses, one has heard, could have been greatly improved by a delay in delivery, and some of them by being delayed indefinitely!

There seems to be a limit placed on the number of speakers who are to engage in oral ministry at this meeting, for we read: "Let the prophets speak two or three, and let the other judge." (See v. 29.)

(g) It should be profitable

No person is a competent judge of the worth of his own ministry, for he is palpably predisposed in his own favor! The principle of scripture is: "Let your prophets speak, and let the other judge" (v. 29). Years ago, a brother had to be approached by the elder brethren with regard to the unprofitable ministry he persisted in inflicting on the long suffering saints. He replied indignantly, "Would you stifle my little ministry?" He then went on to deliver them a lecture, and pointed out that the reason they did not appreciate his ministry was that they were unspiritural, and consequently were not able to recognize good ministry when they heard it!

The late C. F. Hogg used to suggest that the "five words" which Paul would rather speak with his understanding were the words: "What shall I profit you?" These words should challenge every one who rises to speak in a gathering of believers. Each should ask himself, honestly, prayerfully, thoughtfully and sincerely: "Shall what I have to say to this audience be to their spiritual profit?" Many addresses would never have been delivered if this challenge had been honestly faced and a right decision taken.

It is particularly exasperating to hear a speaker say: "The Lord has laid this message on my heart," and then proceed to deliver a most unprofitable discourse. Surely, if the Lord had really given him a message, there would be no need to advertise that fact, for it would become self evident to all who heard, for the hearers should be the best judges as to whether it is from the Lord or not. The effect of prophecy is seen by its profitable effect on the audience. Many imagine that when they have pronounced the magic formula: "The Lord has laid it on my heart," that all adverse criticism is therefore ruled out and definitely not of the Lord!

We have spent some considerable time in discussing this matter of edifying ministry following the breaking of bread, but trust the reader will "suffer the word of exhortation" (Heb. 13:22). We all need to earnestly seek and diligently use the wisdom that only God can give, so that our ministry may be used of Him to accomplish the purpose for which it was given, namely: "The perfecting of the saints for the work of the ministry, for the edifying of the body of Christ" (Eph. 4:12).

5. The principle of harmony and order

At the Lord's supper, as also at all other gatherings of the Lord's people, godly order should prevail. The divine injunction is: "Let all things be done decently and in order" (1 Cor. 14:33, 40). It was the disorder in the Corinthian assembly that occasioned the first epistle, in which Paul rebuked them for their behavior at the Lord's supper, and then proceeded, by means of a special revelation, to lay before them the scriptural order they should henceforth seek to maintain.

This order is not intended to be a mechanical one, or that which comes from strict adherence to an inflexible rule, or a carefully prepared ritual, by which everything is enabled to run with machine-like smoothness. The order is to be a vital and spiritual one, which is to be brought about as each Christian is responsive to the leading of the Holy Spirit as He applies the

Word of God to his heart. In other words, it is the order and harmony that can be observed in an organism, such as the human body. In fact, this is the illustration that is used in the twelfth chapter of this epistle to the Corinthians, where the Church is likened to a human body in which each member fulfils its God-given function, thus making for perfect harmony and edification.

We are therefore justified in coming to the conclusion that where disorder obtains in an assembly, it is not of God, "For God is not the Author of confusion" (1 Cor. 14:33). God's remedy for the disorder that obtained in Corinth was not the substitution of a *different* order of things, but the humble, reverent and sincere subjection to the instructions contained in the Word of God. We have already noted that Christendom has attempted to create an artificial order by arranging the whole service from beginning to end. By this means a certain uniformity is produced, but it is a sorry substitute for the spiritual order that only God can produce as His people are obedient to His leading.

Christians are urged to be "of the same *mind* in the Lord" (Phil. 4:2; 1 Peter 3:8; 1 Cor. 1:10). This must not be interpreted as indicating that all believers must be of the same *opinion*. There may be, and probably is, a great variety of opinion amongst Christians as to the correct interpretation of this verse of Scripture or that. What Paul has in mind here is that they were to be of the same mind regarding the person of Christ, and the fundamental truths of the word of God. Thus there was to be *unity of heart*, without *uniformity of opinion*. It is no wonder that we read: "Behold how good and how pleasant it is for brethren to dwell together in unity!" (Ps. 133:1). As each believer in the assembly fulfills the function for which God has fitted him, there will be that true and vital unity that glorifies the Lord, enriches each believer and edifies the whole assembly. It is only when envy and strife come in that there is "confusion and every evil work" (James 3:16).

Perhaps a practical word in regard to the actual passing of the bread and the cup may also be in order at this point. An embarrassing situation may sometimes arise in a large assembly where two or three hundred believers break bread. Naturally, the size of the congregation will determine both the size of the loaf of bread and the number of plates on which the broken bread is placed, so as to facilitate its passing without undue delay. Where four or more plates are used, each section of the audience is given one plate which is passed to each person in that section, until all have partaken.

It would greatly help if the last brother in each section would hold the plate until all the sections have partaken. Then all these brethren could rise simultaneously and return the plates to the table. In this way all would know that it was now in order for thanks to be given for the cup. This common sense arrangement has proved to be quite helpful, particularly for any visitors who may be present, who may not otherwise know whether *all* the plates have been returned to the table. The same should be done regarding the cups after they have been passed.

Perhaps a word may be in order, at this point, as to the number of cups that should be used at the Lord's supper. As we have noted before, Scripture gives us no hard and fast rules and regulations regarding certain modes of procedure, but rather lays down some broad fundamental *principles* to be kept in mind when coming to a certain conclusion.

Those who insist on a meticulous observance of all the details of the original mode of procedure which our Lord adopted at its institution, will find themselves in a rather difficult position. They would have to go to Jerusalem, gather in an upper room, recline at a table, with only male Jews present, partake of unleavened bread, drink from one cup and sing only the Hallel! Needless to say, this mode of procedure is not insisted on in the New Testament.

As with the bread, after it is broken, the number of plates used to distribute it will be determined by the number of those who are to partake of it; so also will it be in the matter of the number of the cups used. A little thought and the use of arithmetic will soon demonstrate the infeasibility of distributing the elements to a gathering of five hundred or more believers, if only one plate for the bread and one cup for the wine were used.

As all the broken pieces of bread are rightly viewed as being one loaf, seeing they have all been broken from one loaf of bread; so the contents of the various cups used may be rightly viewed as composing one cup, seeing they have all been poured from one container. The number of cups is therefore immaterial. Scripture does not limit the number to one, two, four, eight, or a hundred.

Some assemblies of believers use the individual cup. The use of this method in no wise violates any principle of Scripture. This is a matter which each assembly must be free to decide for itself and, in so doing, should be fully persuaded in its own mind (Rom. 14:5).

Chapter Sixteen

The Procedure of the Lord's Supper:
Order: Obedience, Generosity

6. The principle of obedience

We have seen that Paul, by divine inspiration, gave distinct instructions to the men, both in regard to their behavior and the matter of their oral ministry in the assembly. This called for prompt obedience on the part of each man if the assembly was to be well pleasing to God.

The women also are given particular attention and exhorted to be obedient. First he instructs them in regard to the matter of the necessity for a head covering while in the assembly gathering. He points out that women have two coverings. The first is their hair, which forms a permanent covering. The second is a veil, which is a *temporary* covering, which they are to place on their head when in the assembly (1 Cor. 11:1-16).

Many have argued from verse 15 that the woman's hair is her *sole* covering, and that she does not need to wear a veil, or a hat. A little consideration and the application of common sense will show the absurdity of this contention. If the hair is the covering of the woman, then it must also be the covering of the man. Now look at verse 4, "Every man praying or prophesying, having his head covered, dishonoreth his head." This means that men must uncover their heads when they pray or preach in the assembly.

Now, if the hair is the covering of man's head, as it certainly is; then how can he uncover his head? Must he shave off his hair before he can pray or preach? Of course not, otherwise only bald headed men could pray or preach! Men are to have *uncovered* heads in the assembly gathering, and women are to have *covered* heads in the assembly. (See v. 5.) Therefore, the only conclusion to which we can come is that women are to have an *additional* covering in the shape of a veil or a hat, so that their heads are covered when they meet in the assembly meeting.

Then again, there is the matter of women being distinctly commanded to be silent in the assembly. Note the wording: "Let your women keep silence in the churches, for it is not permitted unto them to speak" (1 Cor. 14:34). Godly women, who desire to be obedient to the "commandments of the Lord" (v. 37), will submit to this, as also to any other commandment recorded in the New Testament scriptures. One woman, when shown this scripture, remarked: "That is only one of *many* matters with which I disagree with the apostle Paul!"

There is also the matter of their preaching and teaching in the assembly. We are definitely told: "I suffer not a woman to teach, nor to unsurp authority over the man, but to be in silence" (1 Tim. 2:12). Yet, in the face of this direct command of the Lord, many women are permitted both to pray and teach in a church gathering, and some denominations actually have ordained women preachers!

We shall not go into the whys and wherefores of this matter of the woman's place in the assembly, for this does not rightly belong to this subject of the Lord's supper, which we are considering particularly. The very fact of its being prohibited in the assembly should be sufficient for all Christian women who wish to obey the Word of God. There is no substitute for obedience. King Saul was reminded of this fact: "To obey is better than sacrifice, and to hearken than the fat of rams" (1 Sam. 15:22).

It is largely the women in the assembly who combine to produce the *spiritual atmosphere* in which the brethren are enabled audibly to take part. If this godly atmosphere is absent, there is a dearth in the land, with its sad consequences. Who can possibly estimate the spiritual value of the presence of these godly women, whose wholehearted submission to the Word of God and wholesouled devotion to the Lord Jesus brings the blessing of the Lord to an assembly of believers!

This does not mean that the women do not have an oral ministry, but it is not to be in the gathering of the saints. Think of their mighty influence in the home as they teach their children. What a sphere they have in the Sunday School, and also in the conduct of women's meetings that have been so greatly blessed of God! More souls have been won to Christ through the ministry of women than through men; but it is ministry in their own sphere. Once a woman leaves that sphere, she is a loser as a result.

7. The principle of generosity

This is found in 1 Corinthians 16:1-2, where Paul deals with the subject of the systematic, proportionate, willing, cheerful and generous giving of one's means to supply the needs of others. Again the expression is found: "Upon the first day of the week." We know that this was the day when the disciples came together to break bread. Thus this collection was also to have its place at the Lord's supper. We therefore have good authority for the collection, which rightly follows the remembrance of the One who, though rich, for our sakes became poor, that we, through His poverty, might be made rich (2 Cor. 8:9).

What a high honor is conferred upon believers that they are able to give to Him, who gave His all for us! Deity delights to give: "God so loved the world that He gave His only begotten Son." The Son of God loved us and gave Himself for us. The Holy Spirit has given Himself to indwell us, and has given to us the holy Scriptures, by His inspiration, and by which He now leads us into all truth. How fitting it is, then, after we have given the Father and the Son our grateful praise and worship, to return to Him some of our substance in the way of money.

One of the evidences of spirituality is generosity. A person may be very sanctimonious and, at the same time be very stingy, but a spiritual person is always generous. The Bible has quite a little to say about giving. In fact, God devotes two whole chapters to this grace of giving. (See 2 Cor. 8 and 9.)

Each Christian is viewed in the New Testament as a steward in a twofold sense. First of all, he has been entrusted with *material possessions* for which, one day, he must give account at the judgment seat of Christ (Rom. 14:10). Then he is described as a steward of the *manifold grace of God* (1 Peter 4:10). To him has been committed the gospel as a sacred trust (1 Tim. 1:11). Every child of God is therefore a debtor to the world to give it the gospel (Rom. 1:14). The solemn words of 1 Corinthians 4:2 should come home to every heart: "It is required in stewards that a man be found faithful." May we be faithful stewards, in both aspects of the term! Now let us think of some of the requirements for the scriptural giving of our means.

(a) It should be proportionate

That is, it should be determined by "what a man has" (2 Cor. 8:12). The wealthy believer is therefore expected to give more than the one with a low income. Under the law, God instructed His people to give at least a tenth of their income to the Lord. It is a good plan for each Christian to determine what percentage of his income shall be ear-marked as the Lord's portion, and then abide by that decision as long as he is able, increasing it if need be. One often hears a believer remark: "All that I have belongs to the

Lord." One feels like asking such: "But how much does the Lord *actually* receive from you?"

(b) It should be systematic

It is a good plan for a Christian to keep an account book, and then carefully note how much he actually gives to the Lord out of the sum total of his income. Some would be unpleasantly surprised, if not shocked, at the large amount they spend on themselves as compared with the small amount they give to the Lord. Like the master of the unjust steward, one day our Lord and Master will say to us: "Give an account of thy stewardship, for thou mayest be no longer steward" (Luke 16:2). This privilege of giving is only ours during our lifetime, so we should take full advantage of the opportunity while it is at our disposal, for "the opportunity of a lifetime must be grasped in the lifetime of the opportunity." If every Christian reading this were to prayerfully determine to become a systematic giver, and then act on his determination, he would soon experience the joy of giving.

(c) It should be willing

God does not desire reluctant giving on the part of His people, but *willing* giving. We learn this from both the Old and the New Testament. In connection with the erection of the Tabernacle, God said to Moses: "Speak unto the children of Israel, that they bring Me an offering: of every man that giveth it willingly with his heart ye shall take My offering" (Ex. 25:2). In 2 Corinthians 8:12 we are told: "If there be first a willing mind, it is accepted according to that a man hath." A farmer was once asked how much milk his cow gave. He replied: "If you're talking in the way of voluntary contributions, she doesn't give any; but if you can get her into a corner and tie her down, you can take three gallons from her!"

In Malachi's day, God charged the people of Israel with having robbed Him. When they inquired: "Wherein have we robbed Thee?" God replied: "In tithes and offerings. Ye are cursed with a curse: for ye have robbed Me, even this whole nation" (Mal. 3:10). Then follows a conditional promise: "Bring ye all the tithes into the storehouse, and prove Me now herewith, saith the Lord of Hosts, if I will not open you the windows of heaven, and pour you out a blessing, that there shall not be room enough to receive it"

(v. 10). God has willingly given to us every good and perfect gift. Best of all, He has given His beloved Son. With such an example of divine generosity we should surely be willing to give to Him. It is good to remember that, in so doing, we are but *returning to Him* a mere fraction of what He has given us. Each believer can therefore say with David: "But who am I, and what is my people that we should be able to offer so willingly after this sort? for all things come of Thee, and of Thine own have we given Thee" (1 Chron. 29:14).

(d) It should be cheerful

We are told that: "God loveth a cheerful giver" (2 Cor. 9:7). The reason is not far to seek: He is a cheerful Giver Himself! It is not for nothing that He is called "the blessed God," or the happy God. Nothing gives God more pleasure than to give, and God has poured multiplied blessings upon us, willingly, freely and bountifully. We should therefore count it the greatest pleasure and honor of our lives to be permitted to give to Him, Who giveth all.

It is one thing to sing heartily the words of that lovely hymn:

> Take my silver and my gold,
> Not a mite would I withhold;

but an entirely different thing to do it. It is recorded in Mark 12:41 that, "Jesus sat over against the treasury, and beheld how the people cast money into the treasury." It might be a good exercise of soul if every believer could visualize the Lord Jesus looking over his shoulder, as the offering basket is passed, to see what proportion of his income is placed in the container.

Someone has written:

> Give as you would if an angel
> Awaited your gift at the door.
> Give as you would if tomorrow
> Found you where giving was o'er.
> Give as you would to the Master,
> If you met His loving look.
> Give as you would of your substance,
> If His hand your offering took.

(e) It should be intelligent

Every Christian is entitled to know where his money is going. This is the day of countless appeals for money. One has only to open some of the religious magazines to be deluged with eloquent appeals for the support of this mission or that work. Doubtless, most of these missions are seeking to preach the gospel. What is the Christian to do? He cannot give to all.

A believer's first responsibility is to support his own home assembly. There are certain obligations that must be met, in the cost of the building and its necessary upkeep in the way of heat, light and repairs. Then there is the question of gospel activity, such as the Family Bible Hour, the Sunday School, the gospel meeting, etc.

Believers should also remember that the necessary expenses for the upkeep of the meeting place, and the services in connection with the assembly, continue whether they are there or not. The fact that a believer is on vacation does not relieve him of his responsibility in this matter. He should therefore make arrangements that, during his absence, his regular contribution for the support of the assembly should be kept up, so that the collection from the saints will not suffer as a result of his bodily absence.

Then there is the matter of helping the poor, the incapacitated, the sick, etc. Added to this there is the financial support of full time workers who have been invited to come and minister the Word. Nor should the needs of the foreign missionary be forgotten. These men have gone forth, at the Lord's command, to a foreign country, looking alone to the Lord for their support. They make no public appeals for money. Not only so, but they are seeking to carry out the scriptural principles of gathering in their field of labor. Thus there is a great need for the proportionate, systematic, willing and cheerful giving on the part of each believer if these, and other needs, are to be met. If every Christian gave as he should, there would be no shortage of material supplies, either in the homeland or in the foreign field.

Seeing it is the Lord's money, Christians should seek to invest it wisely, where they know it will be used to the best possible advantage to further the interests of the greatest business on earth—the Lord's business. It is to be feared that many give carelessly, on the impulse of the moment, without due regard as to what the money will be used for. In many cases, due to an eloquently worded appeal, money has actually been given to support a work that is not being conducted along scriptural lines. We are told that: "Charity begins at home." We should therefore exercise intelligence in our giving, and be loyal in our support of those persons who are seeking, not only to preach the gospel, but are also engaged in the work of teaching converts to "observe all things" which the Lord has commanded (Matt. 28:19-20).

Those who have gone forth on scriptural lines do not advertise their needs, either privately or publicly, by an eloquent oral or a well-worded written appeal. These make known their needs to God alone and He, in turn, supplies them through the gifts of His people. These are the ones, therefore, that should have first claim on the support of those who profess to believe in these same scriptural principles.

Each believer therefore should be much exercised before the Lord, not only as to how much he should give, but also as to how this money should be invested. In this way he will be an *intelligent* giver. The question asked by the unjust steward of his master's debtors may appropriately be addressed to each Christian: "How much owest thou my Lord?" (Luke 16:5). Each believer is a debtor both to God and to his fellow man. May it be true of each reader that he pays what he owes. Happy indeed is that assembly of which it can be truthfully said, as Paul said of the Macedonian believers: "How that, in a great trial of affliction, the abundance of their joy and their deep poverty abounded unto the riches of their liberality" (2 Cor. 8:2).

(f) It should be evidenced by hospitality

While on the subject of generosity it may not be amiss to say a word about the attractive grace of hospitality. This is one of the marks of a true elder, for he is described as being "given to hospitality" (1 Tim. 3:2). Nor is this grace to be confined to elders, for we read: "Be not forgetful to entertain strangers, for thereby some have entertained angels unawares" (Heb. 13:2). It is easy to become self centered and self occupied, and think only in terms of our own comfort and convenience, and give little or no thought to the comfort and convenience of others.

Here is a Christian who has newly arrived in a city and is staying at a hotel. He comes to the Lord's supper and his letter of commendation is read. How nice it would be if, after the meeting, the saints would personally welcome him, and that someone would invite him to his home for dinner. What a welcome change it would be for him from the cold atmosphere of a hotel, with no Christian fellowship. Wonderful friendships have been formed in this way that have changed the course of a person's life for, in so doing, they have "entertained angels unawares."

The tendency is for Christians to leave all this entertaining to one or two of the more well to do in the assembly, but surely this is both the privilege and responsibility of any believer, whatever his station in life may be, or however humble may be his home. It is quite true that there is a measure of inconvenience in entertaining strangers, but the reward more than compensates for the effort.

All of us would be overjoyed if we had the opportunity of entertaining the Lord Jesus in our home, as did Mary, Martha and Lazarus. Well, we can do it today by entertaining the Lord's people, for our Savior said: "Inasmuch as ye have done it unto one of the least of these My brethren, ye have done it unto Me" (Matt. 25:40). Of some believers it was written: "God is not unrighteous to forget your work and labor of love which ye have shown towards His name, in that ye have ministered unto the saints, and do minister" (Heb. 6:10). May the Lord speak to our hearts in this very important matter.

Many a Christian soldier, far from home, who has never heard of assemblies of believers who meet on scriptural lines, has been brought by a fellow Christian to the Lord's supper. There he was warmly welcomed to the breaking of bread and then, after the meeting, was entertained in the home of one of the saints and made to feel at home. Then the Scriptures have been opened to him in a wise and courteous fashion, and the truth of the Church brought before him. As a result, many such have been led to see their privilege to meet in Christ's name alone, apart from the denominational barriers that men have erected. Many are now in happy fellowship with such companies of the Lord's people, and daily thank God that their footsteps were ever directed to such a gathering. The grace of hospitality is not the least of the graces that should characterize those who are saved by grace.

Chapter Seventeen

The Day and the Frequency of the Lord's Supper:
Day of Observance

We now come to the matter as to the day on which the Lord's supper is to be celebrated, and also how frequently it should be observed. We shall think of four things in this connection. First, the day of its observance. Second, the time of its observance. Third, the length of the meeting. Fourth, the frequency with which it should be observed.

The Day of its Observance

There is a day in the New Testament which is distinguished from all other days of the week by the title: "The Lord's day" (Rev. 1:10). This is also spoken of as: "the first day of the week." This expression occurs quite often. It was the day on which our Lord rose triumphant from the dead, a day of resurrection (Luke 24:1). It was the day when the Lord appeared to His disciples in the upper room (John 20:19). It was the day when, a week later, He again appeared to His disciples, this time with Thomas present. Note, it was "eight days after," that is, the first day of the week (John 20:26). It was on this day that the disciples came together to break bread (Acts 20:7). It was the day on which Christians were to give to the Lord that which they had purposed in their hearts to place in the collection (1 Cor. 16:2). It was the day when the Church came into existence, for it was on the day of Pentecost that this great event took place. (See Lev. 23:15-21; Acts 2:1.)

The Lord's supper, as we have seen, was not instituted on the first day of the week, but three days before. Why, then, is the first day of the week selected as the day on which the early Church observed the Lord's supper? The answer is plain: it was the day on which our Lord Jesus rose from the dead. By this, our Lord introduced into the world something which had not previously existed, namely, Christianity.

For over two thousand years, Israel, under the law, had observed the Sabbath day, which was the seventh day of the week. We are told that the Sabbath constituted a sign between God and Israel. We read: "Verily, My sabbaths ye shall keep, for it is a sign between Me and you throughout your generations: that ye may know that I am the Lord that doth sanctify you" (Ex. 31:13). Again we are told, "It is a sign between Me and the children of Israel forever" (v. 16). Thus the Sabbath belongs exclusively to Israel, and was never given to the Church to observe. In fact, the third commandment of the law, regarding the strict observance of the Sabbath day, is the only one that is not repeated in the New Testament.

It is falsely asserted by the Seventh Day Adventists that the Roman Catholics changed the Sabbath day from the seventh day of the week to the first day of the week. The falsity of this claim is seen in the fact that long before the Roman Catholic church came into existence, the first day of the week was being regularly observed by Christians. One has only to read a reliable Church History to verify this fact. The early Church Fathers, those who lived immediately after the apostles, have left behind written records which furnish us with interesting information regarding the history of the post-apostolic years. Barnabas (AD 100), Ignatius (AD 107), Justin Martyr (AD 145-150) and Irenaeus (AD 155-202) all speak of the first day of the week as the day when believers met together to remember the Lord.

There is definite scriptural proof that it was not the Roman Catholic Church, but God who changed the day from the Sabbath to the Lord's day. In Psalm 118:22-24 we read: "The stone which the builders refused is become the headstone of the corner. This is the Lord's doing; it is marvelous in our eyes. This is the day which the Lord hath made; we will be glad and rejoice in it." There is no doubt whatever as to the Messianic character of this prophecy. Our Lord quoted it as referring to Himself. (See Matt. 21:42; Mark 12:10-12; Luke 20:17-19.) Peter also used this same scripture to drive home to the leaders of Israel their awful sin in having crucified the Lord of glory. (See Acts 4:10-12.)

When did God take the Stone, which the builders refused, and make Him the head stone of the corner? The answer is clear: "As it began to dawn towards the first day of the week" (Matt. 28:1). The resurrection of Christ, on the first day of the week, thus became: "The day which the Lord hath made." Well may we be glad and rejoice in it! Be sure of this, the Roman Catholics had nothing whatever to do with the making of this day, it was done by God Himself, and this in fulfilment of a prophecy given a thousand years before the Son of God became incarnate! Let us think of three things that mark the Lord's day, or the first day of the week, as being distinctively characteristic of Christianity.

1. It was a day of victorious resurrection

Our Lord had declared, time and again, that He was to be crucified and that He would rise from the dead on the third day (Matt. 16:21, 20:18-19; Mark 8:31, 9:31; Luke 18:33). This fact was also known to His enemies, for we are told that after the death of Christ the chief priests went to Pilate and said: "Sir, we remember that that deceiver said, while He was yet alive, 'After three days I will rise again;' Command therefore that the sepulchre be made sure until the third day, lest His disciples come by night and steal Him away, and say unto the people: 'He is risen from the dead!'" How strange it seems that the enemies of Christ remembered what His disciples forgot! (See Matt. 27:62-64; John 20:9; Luke 24:10-11).

With this knowledge of Christ's intention, His enemies did their utmost to make certain His body would never emerge from that tomb. A huge stone was rolled before its entrance, an official seal was placed upon that stone and a guard of men was employed to watch the tomb day and night.

How graphically Matthew describes the events of that most wonderful first day of the week. Let us note the words carefully: "In the end of the Sabbath, as it began to dawn toward the first day of the week, came Mary Magdalene and the other Mary to see the sepulchre. And behold, there was a great earthquake: for the angel of the Lord descended from heaven, and came and rolled back the stone from the door and sat upon it. His countenance was like lightning, and his raiment white as snow: and for fear of him the keepers did shake, and became as dead men. And the angel answered and said unto the women, 'Fear not ye: for I know that ye seek Jesus which was crucified. He is not here: for He is risen, as He said. Come, see the place where the Lord lay. And go quickly, and tell His disciples that He is risen from the dead; and, behold, He goeth before you into Galilee; there shall ye see Him: lo, I have told you'" (Matt. 28:1-7).

Thus, in fulfilment of His own word, He, who had laid down His life, took it up again, henceforth to live in the power of an endless life. How blessed it is to know that: "Christ, being raised from the dead, dieth no more; death hath no more dominion over Him. In that He died, He died unto sin once (for all): but in that He liveth, He liveth unto God" (Rom. 6:10; John 10:17-18). He, who in infinite grace, stooped to the dust of death for our sins, rose victorious from the grave, ascended to heaven, and is now glorified at the right hand of the majesty on high, awaiting the time when His enemies shall become the footstool of His feet (Ps. 2:1-8). Yes, the

Lord Jesus is the mighty Conqueror over sin, death and Satan! No wonder, therefore, that the first day of the week is a day never to be forgotten!

2. It was a day of divine vindication

The resurrection was God's "Amen," to Christ's "It is finished!" It was God's imprimatur, or seal of approval, on everything His beloved Son had ever said or done. Every claim that Christ had made was substantiated by the resurrection. He had declared Himself to be the Son of God and, as such, had claimed equality with God; and worthy of equal honor with the Father (John 5:22-23). Was His claim true? The resurrection proves it beyond the shadow of a doubt. Every other statement He made is also authenticated by the fact that He rose from the dead.

(a) The Father's endorsement

It is the Father's endorsement of the fact that all the work needed for the salvation of every sinner had been accomplished to His complete satisfaction (Rom. 4:25).

(b) Proof of Christ's Deity

It is the incontestable proof of Christ's essential and eternal Deity, as equal and eternal with the Father and the Holy Spirit. We are told he was "Declared to be the Son of God with power, according to the Spirit of holiness by the resurrection from the dead" (Rom. 1:4).

(c) Demonstration of truth of His words

It is the endorsement of the truth of all His words. Think of those wonderful statements He made, as found in the four Gospels. Take John 3:16; 5:24; 10:9; 10:27-30, etc. He had stated He was "the way, the truth, and the life," and that no one could come unto the Father but by Him (John 14:6). Was this statement the truth, the whole truth, and nothing but the truth? Yes, indeed. A risen, glorified Man in heaven bears eloquent testimony to this fact. Mark the tremendous statement recorded in John 12:47-48, "If any man hear My words, and believe not, I judge him not: for I came not to judge the world, but to save the world. He that rejecteth Me, and receiveth not My words, hath one that judgeth him: the word that

I have spoken, the same shall judge him in the last day." The fact that a person does not believe the words of Christ in no wise affects their truth. Denying facts does not disprove them, but only reveals the folly of the unbeliever. Jesus said: "Heaven and earth shall pass away, but My words shall never pass away" (Matt. 24:35).

(d) Measure of believer's power

It is the measure of the power that God has placed at the disposal of the believer, for we read: "That ye may know what is the exceeding greatness of His power to usward who believe, according to the working of His mighty power which He wrought in Christ, when He raised Him from the dead" (Eph. 1:18-20). Thus the believer has, in Christ, an illimitable supply of power sufficient to meet all his requirements on earth.

(e) Pledge and pattern of resurrection

It is both the pledge and pattern of the resurrection and glorification of all those who believe on Him. Our Lord declared: "Because I live, ye shall live also" (John 14:19). Because the grave was not the end of His history, so death will not terminate the history of those who believe in Him. This is the argument of 1 Thessalonians 4:14-18; and 1 Corinthians 15:19-23.

(f) Assurance Christ is Judge

It is the assurance God has given that Christ shall be the ultimate Judge of all humanity. We are told that: "God commandeth all men everywhere to repent, because He hath appointed a day in the which He will judge the world in righteousness by that Man whom He hath ordained: whereof He hath given assurance unto all men, in that He hath raised Him from the dead" (Acts 17:30-31). Thus every unbeliever, Christ rejecter and salvation neglecter, who dies in that condition, shall one day have to face Christ as his Judge and hear from Him the dread sentence of eternal banishment from His presence. See John 5:22; Revelation 20:11-15.

(g) Guarantee Christ will be King

It is the guarantee that Christ shall yet be "the King of kings and Lord of lords," and that, "at the name of Jesus, every knee shall bow, and every tongue confess that He is Lord, to the glory of God the Father" (Phil 2:8-11; Rev. 11:15). Thus the universe shall yet own the absolute sovereignty of the Son of God. Happy indeed are those who have bowed the knee to Him in time, trusted Him as Savior and owned Him as the Lord of their lives! Yes, the first day of the week is "the day which the Lord hath made," and we do well to be "glad and rejoice in it!"

3. It is a day of grateful commemoration.

It is the day when believers come together, at His invitation, to remember Him in the observance of the Lord's supper. From Acts 20:6-7 we learn that Paul, though in a hurry to get to Jerusalem, waited seven days in Troas in order to observe the Lord's supper on the first day of the week. Here is clear evidence that this was the day the early Church broke bread. From the dawn of Christianity unto this present day, there have been companies of Christians, often few in number because of persecution, who have gathered together in His name to remember Him. Thus, through the years, there has been this testimony for Him. It has been like an oasis in the desert to these companies who have maintained their witness to Him in this way in that spiritually barren wilderness called the world.

In the early days, it was in the deep catacombs of Rome that, by the light of a candle, the Christians came to show forth the death of their beloved Lord. All down the ages there has been this testimony for Christ, in scriptural simplicity, and in humble dependence on Him, and with the word of God as their sole authority, these groups have taken the bread and the cup and thus fulfilled their Lord's request. They hail the coming of this day with great delight, for they are to be the guests of none other than the Son of God, who is to be in their midst according to His own promise. As they meet they sing that beautiful hymn:

> With Jesus in our midst,
> We gather 'round the board;
> Though many, we are one in Christ,
> One body in the Lord.
>
> (R. C. Chapman)

Chapter Eighteen

The Day and the Frequency of the Lord's Supper:
Time, Length, Frequency of Observance

The Time of its Observance

Inasmuch as no particular time of the day has been designated in the New Testament as being necessary for its observance, this matter is of no consequence. It is true that it was instituted in the evening, but this was due to the fact that it followed the Passover feast, which was kept "between the evenings" (Ex. 12:6). Some have argued from this that the Lord's supper must also be observed in the evening, or it is not "scriptural." In fact, we sometimes hear of certain Christians, gifted with hair splitting propensities, who refuse to break bread unless it is done in the evening!

In the early days of Christianity, the evening was the most convenient time for the majority of the brethren to come together. Many of the believers were slaves, who were owned by unsaved masters. Consequently they could only come after their duties were over for the day. Doubtless it was in the evening that Paul and the disciples met at Troas, for Paul preached until midnight, and it is hardly probable that he preached all day long! Then again, in times of persecution, the believers had to meet secretly, for it was a crime to be a Christian in those days. To be discovered at such a meeting meant imprisonment and death; consequently darkness was the best time to gather to remember the Lord in the breaking of bread.

Nowadays, of course, we are not faced with such conditions. The first day of the week is a public holiday, and most assemblies have found that the morning is the most convenient time for the majority of Christians to gather. The time, therefore, will be determined by the conditions that obtain in the area where the believers live. With some it may be in the morning, while with others, the afternoon is best. Some may find the evening is the ideal time. When determining the time, it should ever be kept in mind that the Lord's supper is the principal meeting of the whole week, therefore the very best time should be reserved for it.

As to the Length of the Meeting

Again the New Testament furnishes us with no information on this score. We do know that the principal purpose for which they came together was the breaking of bread, but how long the meeting lasted is not known. In some denominations the Lord's supper is observed only once a month or even less frequently. Often it is announced to follow the main preaching service, and those interested are invited to remain for "holy communion." This is usually a very short and sparsely attended service. Thus, what should have been the principal meeting of the week is relegated to a place of secondary importance, and made a mere appendage to the preaching service.

Inasmuch as we are living in an age governed largely by the clock, therefore it is necessary to determine beforehand what period of time shall be devoted to this meeting, so as to permit time for any ministry of the Word that may follow. Again, circumstances will determine largely how long a period it should be. In some assemblies the Family Bible Hour follows the breaking of bread, with a little interval between. Other assemblies have their Sunday School in the afternoon, and this permits a later starting time in the morning for the Lord's supper.

It would seem that an hour and a half, or an hour and a quarter is the average time assigned to the remembrance meeting. Where the Sunday School follows this meeting, it will be necessary to keep to the time limit, or confusion will result.

Visiting preachers should be informed when the meeting should end, so that they may be guided accordingly as to any ministry they may bring. In some meeting rooms there is a sign, tastefully designed and hung where all can see, which reads: "For the benefit of our visitors, this meeting should end by ____________." This seems to be a very common sense arrangement, and is calculated to save any speaker from the embarrassment of prolonging the meeting beyond its appointed time limit.

The Frequency of its Observance

The question is often raised as to how often the Lord's supper should be observed. Some believe it should take place each Lord's day, while others celebrate it once a month. Still others, once a quarter, while some advise twice a year. Some never observe it at all. The Salvation Army do not partake of the Lord's supper, nor do they practice believers' baptism. The same is true of the Society of Friends, or Quakers. They believe that Christ only intended this ordinance to be observed in a spiritual way, in heart communion with Him, in the sense of Revelation 3:20.

While Scripture does not give us any plain and definite command as to how often it should be observed, we can gather from the example of the early church that it was their custom to meet each Lord's day for this purpose. We have already seen that Acts 2:46 indicates it was observed each day in the homes of individual Christians, but that, later on, it became a weekly observance as indicated in Acts 20:7. It is mentioned as being the common practice of that day. The same expression is found in 1 Corinthians 16:2: "Upon the first day of the week," indicating it was the custom of the believers at Corinth to come together each Lord's day to remember the Lord. It does not say: "On the first Lord's day of the month," or "the first Lord's day of the quarter." Those who object to the weekly observance of the Lord's supper certainly have no objection to taking a collection each first day of the week! If it is true of the one, it is also true of the other.

In 1 Corinthians 11:26 we read: "As *often* as ye eat this bread and drink this cup." This surely indicates that it was not *seldom* observed. In Acts 2:41-42 we are told that they who "gladly received the word . . . continued stedfastly in . . . the breaking of bread." Thus it was not a spasmodic thing, but a stedfast continuance in its observation that is indicated by these words. From this pattern found in the New Testament, we therefore conclude that it was observed each Lord's day, at a time most convenient to all. The exhortation of Heb. 10:25 ought to have a voice for each believer: "Not forsaking the assembling of ourselves together as the manner of some is: and so much the more as ye see the day (of Christ's coming) approaching."

Some years ago an older Christian, while discussing the matter of church truth with a younger believer, mentioned that he met each Lord's day with believers to observe the Lord's supper. The young believer looked his astonishment and inquired incredulously: "You mean you take communion every Lord's day?" "Yes," replied the other: "We break bread each Sunday." At this the young man remarked: "Apparently you have forgotten that old adage, 'Familiarity breeds contempt.' Why, a rite so often repeated is apt to lose all its significance and value."

Then, warming up to his subject he continued: "I would suggest that you take communion once a month. Better still, once every three months.

Still better, twice a year; but best of all, once a year. Think with what expectation you would look forward to taking the Lord's supper if you knew that twelve months had to elapse between these great occasions! Why, you would look forward to it with the same glad anticipation that children do to Christmas day!" And so he went on.

When he was through, the older man, knowing that his friend was an only son and that he was away from home at the time, inquired: "I understand you have a father and mother who love you very much. Is this true?" "Yes," replied the young man, "they certainly love me." "And do you love them ?" was his next question. "I certainly do," was the young man's reply. Then came the next question: "How often do they write to you, and you to them?" He replied: "Twice a week."

The older man remarked: "Apparently you have forgotten the old adage that 'Familiarity breeds contempt.' Why, this idea of writing home so often is apt to lose all its significance and value. I would suggest that they write you once a month, better still, once every three months; still better, twice a year; but best of all, once a year. Think with what eager expectation they would look forward to getting a letter from you, and you from them, if twelve months had to elapse between these great occasions! Why, you would look forward to it with the same eagerness as children do to Christmas!" The young man saw where his argument had led him, and changed the subject!

Can you imagine a young man who has courted the affections of a young woman, and has obtained her acceptance of his proposal of marriage, complaining to a friend: "Must I go and see her once a week? Wouldn't once a month be sufficient?" Do we really love the Lord Jesus? If so, we shall not be thinking of how *seldom* we can remember Him in the way He has requested, but how *often* we are privileged to do so. Surely once a week is not too often to remember the One we profess to love above all others and who, in His wonderful grace, bore our sins and suffered all the judgment of a holy God in our stead, and rose to be our Lord and very best Friend.

The writings of the early fathers serve to confirm the fact, if further confirmation is needed, of this weekly observance of the Lord's supper. Thus we affirm it is the privilege of the Lord's people, each Lord's day, to come together in the Lord's name, and with the Lord in their midst, in the Lord's own appointed way, to partake of the Lord's supper, in remembrance of the Lord Jesus, and thus show forth the Lord's death until the Lord comes back again. May it be ours to take full advantage of this priceless privilege of thus fulfilling the desire of our blessed Lord when He said, on the night of His betrayal, "This do for a remembrance of Me."

Here are two quotations, the first from Jonathan Edwards, written two hundred years ago. The other is from one of the greatest preachers the world has ever known, C. H. Spurgeon. Both have a word as to the frequency of the Lord's supper.

> "It seems plain by the Scripture, that the primitive Christians were wont to celebrate this memorial of the sufferings of their dear Redeemer every Lord's day: and so I believe it will be again in the Church of Christ in days that are approaching."
>
> –Jonathan Edwards
>
> "My witness is, and I think I speak the mind of many of God's people now present, that coming as some of us do, weekly, to the Lord's table, we do not find the breaking of bread to have lost its significance—it is always fresh to us. I have often remarked, on Lord's day evening, whatever the subject may have been, whether Sinai has thundered over our heads, or the plaintive notes of Calvary have pierced our hearts, it always seems equally appropriate to come to the breaking of bread. Shame on the Christian Church that she should put it off to once a month, and mar the first day of the week by depriving it of its glory in the meeting together for fellowship and breaking of bread, and showing forth the death of Christ till He come. Those who know the sweetness of each Lord's day celebrating His Supper will not be content, I am sure, to put it off to less frequent seasons."
>
> –C. H. Spurgeon

Chapter Nineteen

The Christian's Responsibility to the Lord's Supper:
Be Present

We have discussed the institution, the symbolism, the purpose, the participants, the procedure, and the day and frequency of the Lord's supper. Now we are to consider the matter of our responsibility to it. We have seen what a great privilege and honor it is to be present at the ordinance which our Lord instituted on the eve of Calvary; but privilege brings with it a corresponding responsibility. Our Lord declared: "If ye know these things, happy are ye if ye do them" (John 13:17). To *know* what the Lord would have us to do is one thing, and to *do* it is another. It would be far better not to know His will than to know it and not do it. What should be the response of each believer who has seen, from the New Testament scriptures, the desire of the Lord Jesus for him to observe the Lord's supper?

To Be Present Himself

This may sound obvious, but with many believers it is not quite so obvious as it appears, for it seems that the least cause is deemed sufficient for them to absent themselves from the Lord's supper. Reasons that would never keep them from going to work on Monday morning are viewed as sufficient to prevent them from attending the meeting for the breaking of bread on Sunday morning. It may be a slight headache, perhaps a light rain, a chilly morning, or a little snow and ice on the streets, or they may not "feel like going." On Monday morning, these would not have the slightest deterrent effect on them. It is only on Sunday that these take upon themselves a different and more serious aspect. It leads one to wonder whether the amount of money in the pay envelope, at the end of the week, could possibly be the determining factor in causing them to leave their comfortable homes and brave the inclement elements on Monday morning.

Someone has facetiously described this as a disease called, "Morbus Sabbaticus," or Sunday sickness. No symptoms whatever are felt on Saturday night. The patients sleep well and eat a very hearty breakfast. As the time of the meeting approaches, this strange disease suddenly attacks them. They don't "feel well," so consequently stay home. Strangely enough, the attack completely disappears at noon, and the patients are able to eat a big dinner, take a nap and a walk and eat a good supper. As the time for the evening meeting approaches, however, there is another seizure of this strange disease, so that once again they do not feel able to venture out, so make themselves comfortable at home. Peculiarly enough, all the symptoms disappear by around nine o'clock, and they are able to sleep well. They awaken on Monday morning and are entirely free from the disease for the rest of the week, until the next Lord's day, and again the attack comes at the same time and with the same results. It never lasts longer than twenty-four hours, and only comes on Sunday, but it works havoc with the believer's spiritual life. Let all Christians beware of "Morbus Sabbaticus!"

If everybody stayed at home each time he had a slight headache, or a little twinge of pain, or it was a cold, blustery morning, what would happen to business? Only that excuse which can bear the light of the judgment seat of Christ should be allowed to stand in the way of a believer's weekly attendance at the Lord's supper. To use a flimsy excuse for absenting himself from this meeting is a sure indication of a lack of heart, and an absence of spirituality on the part of that person.

Sometimes the arrival of an unexpected visitor is allowed to interfere with one's attendance at the remembrance feast. Let us use a "suppose" illustration to clarify what we have in mind. We will suppose that a Christian couple, living in Washington, D. C., have received an invitation from the President to have supper with him at the White House. The invitation is accepted and adequate preparations are made for the great event. The supper is to be at 7 P. M. Just as they are about to leave for the White House, the door bell rings. On opening the door, there stands Uncle Ebenezer and Aunt Jemima, from Podunk, Iowa, who have decided to pay their favorite nephew a surprise visit. Now what will this couple do under these circumstances? Will they call up the President and ask to be excused from attending the supper because of the unexpected visit; or will they explain the situation to their relatives, and ask them to make themselves at home until they return from the presidential supper? The answer will surely be that, while they are very glad to see their relatives, they will not allow this to interfere with their attendance at the White House supper.

Now let us apply our illustration. The Lord Jesus Christ, the King of kings and the Lord of lords, has invited this same couple to His supper. As they are about to leave, the door bell rings, and there is Uncle Ebenezer and Aunt Jemima, who have paid an unexpected visit. What will happen now? Will they forgo the Lord's supper in order to entertain their unexpected guests, or will they explain the situation to their guests, and ask them to make themselves at home until they return from the Lord's supper? It will all depend on their estimation of the Lord Jesus as to who shall have the preference: the Lord of glory, or their relatives.

Which supper should be deemed the most important, the President's or the Lord's? It is to be feared that often the Lord's supper is relegated to a place of secondary importance by the arrival of visitors. Thus friends and relatives are given priority over the Son of God! These things ought not so to be. The Lord Jesus must always and ever have the preeminence, and His invitation: "This do for a remembrance of Me," must come before all else, for "a King's request is His command."

Now let us imagine another situation. This same couple is invited to the home of a Christian friend one Saturday for a social evening. Unfortunately, the party does not break up until after midnight. Consequently, instead of rising at the usual hour on Sunday morning, they oversleep and discover, to their dismay, that there is no time to get ready and be present at the Lord's supper. Thus a social gathering, which is perfectly right in itself, has been allowed to rob them of the privilege of being present at the remembrance meeting. Doubtless we have all discovered that it is possible for the good to become the enemy of the best. The words of Ps. 127:2 are surely in order in this connection: "It is vain for you to rise up early and sit up late, to eat the bread of sorrows."

The Christian should therefore carefully watch his Saturday nights, if he expects to be at his best on Sunday morning. It is simply a case of giving the priority where it belongs—to the Lord. It is important, therefore, to get to bed on time if we are to be at our best physically, mentally and spiritually on the Lord's day. The Lord's supper is surely not the place for yawning and sleepiness, because we have failed, for want of thought, to get the necessary sleep the night before.

Still another cause for absenteeism is the fact that sometimes the wife stays home to cook a sumptuous repast for the family, and thus she is not present at the Lord's supper. One recalls a Christian couple who, from the day of their wedding, decided they would rather eat a cold meal on Sunday noon rather than one of them should miss the remembrance feast. They kept this up all the long years of their married life. They did quite a little entertaining of the Lord's people. All their guests were delighted to go to their home and enjoy their hospitality, the more so because they knew it had not kept their hostess from the Lord's supper.

It is possible, as we all know, to be too busy for God. Martha is not the only sister who has been "cumbered about with much serving" (Luke 10:40). Most people would be far better off with less to eat at Sunday noon, for a large meal and mental alertness do not go hand in hand! The reader can possibly think of many more situations which can arise to prevent the Lord's people from being where they should each Lord's day.

Sometimes a believer is absent from the Lord's supper because he has received and accepted an invitation to speak to some denominational group at the same time as the meeting for the remembrance of the Lord Jesus in his own home assembly. Consequently his seat is empty, and he is missing from the trysting place of his Lord and Savior, and thus fails to respond to the request: "This do for a remembrance of Me."

While no one will belittle the importance of preaching the gospel whenever or wherever it is possible, or attempt to draw up a rigid set of rules and regulations as to when and where a Christian may or may not go and teach the word of God; yet the advisibility of this course of action is open to question.

The New Testament clearly indicates that each believer is a servant of the Lord Jesus and, as such, is responsible alone to his Lord and Master for both the character and sphere of his service for Him. It is written: "Who art thou that judgest another man's servant? To his own Master he standeth or falleth" (Rom. 14:4).

It must also be kept in mind that, to the Christian, "all things are *lawful*," yet it must also be remembered that "all things are not *expedient*" for him (1 Cor. 6:12). The Christian must not only be able to distinguish between the good and the bad, but he must also learn to differentiate between that which is *good* and that which is *best*; for it is possible for the good to become the *enemy* of the best.

Each believer should therefore weigh carefully and prayerfully, in the presence of God, and be "fully persuaded in his own mind" as to the relative value of his service for God and the greater value of his worship to God. He should lay to heart the fact that service for the Lord should never be at the *expense* of his worship of the Lord, and that the supper ordained by his Lord should have precedence over any service rendered for Him.

While we know there is no definite and authoritative *command*, on the part of the Lord Jesus, for His disciples to partake of the Lord's supper each Lord's day, yet each Christian should frankly face three facts. First, the definite request of His Lord to remember Him in the breaking of the bread and the drinking of the cup. Second, the example of the early Christians who sought to meet together each Lord's day to partake of the Lord's supper. Third, the unspeakable privilege of thus meeting, in the presence of the Lord Himself, with one's fellow believers, to fulfil the gracious desire of the Lord Jesus Christ: "This do for a remembrance of Me." With these three things in his mind, the believer should have no hesitation in making his choice between being present at the Lord's supper, or being absent from it because of some service for Him.

In this connection, we cannot do better than quote the words of a well known and able teacher of the Word of God, Mr. C. F. Hogg, of London, England. "A man may use what he conceives to be his liberty to the full, going hither and thither to preach, but by so doing he dissipates his energies and builds nothing; or he may surrender his liberty of movement, so to speak, and thus preserve his liberty to declare the whole counsel of God, and to build up a church of God, teaching the saints to observe all things whatsoever he himself has learned of God. In view of the terms of our commission, and the example of the apostle, there seems little room for hesitation as to which is the better path" (Matt. 28:18-19; Acts 20:20, 27).

Surely it should go without saying that if the assembly, of which we form a part, is scriptural in its principles of gathering, then each believer should seek to support it loyally, by all the means in his power, by his presence, prayers and gifts. It is possible for a believer to become so involved in Christian work, under denominational auspices, that he has no time to fulfil his obligations to his own home assembly. Thus he *dissipates* his energies instead of *concentrating* them, and only succeeds in spreading himself so thin that he gets nowhere.

The ancient Romans had a saying that is well worthy of consideration: "Do nothing which, if done by all, would injure the state." Supposing all the brethren in an assembly absented themselves from the Lord's supper in order to accept an invitation to preach elsewhere; what would happen to the meeting for the remembrance of the Lord Jesus? The words of the inspired apostle are appropriate in this connection: "And this I pray, that your love may abound yet more and more in knowledge and in all judgment; that ye may approve things that are excellent (or, try the things which differ), that ye may be sincere and without offence till the day of Christ" (Phil. 1:9-10).

Both the world, the flesh and the Devil will combine to hinder the Christian from being in his place at the Lord's supper. Many Christians, when laid aside through sickness, have confessed how little they realized the value of the remembrance feast until they could not go to it, even though they would have liked to be present. The same is true of those who are in the armed forces of our country. Let each believer determine that, by the grace of God, and as far as lies in his power, he will be present each first day of the week to keep tryst with his Lord and Savior, and enjoy this "sweet feast of love divine."

Chapter Twenty

The Christian's Responsibility to the Lord's Supper:
Be on Time, Prepared, Reverent, Concentrating

To Be There on Time

Here is where many fail, chiefly from the want of a little forethought, and the application of some common sense. How often the worship of the Lord's people has been disturbed by those who *habitually* come late. We are not referring to those occasions when, through circumstances beyond our control, we are unavoidably detained. We are thinking particularly of those that arise from a failure to do a little sensible planning. By the use of a little planning, plus a good dose of resolution, backed up by some practical action, this can and should be avoided.

The Lord Jesus is our Example in this respect also, for we read: "When the hour was come, He sat down and the twelve apostles with Him" (Luke 22:14). Habitual tardiness is surely inexcusable. It shows a slovenly disposition, a lack of common courtesy, honesty and decency. What right has this brother or sister to rob his fellow Christians of the time which they have set apart for the remembrance of the Lord and worship, by rudely interrupting their thoughts as they make their tardy and sometimes noisy entrance? These people get to work on time on Monday morning, for some of them have to punch a clock. In business, habitual lateness will result in unwelcome repercussions from their employer. Why should the Lord be treated with less respect than an earthly employer?

Such chronic lateness also indicates a lack of self control, and an inability to discipline oneself to meet certain legitimate requirements. It connotes both physical, mental and spiritual slothfulness, together with a carelessness that almost amounts to callousness for the feelings of others. It is the very quintessence of inconsideration, for it has no regard for the convenience or feelings of others. Thus they come, five, ten, fifteen and even twenty minutes late, disturbing all by their entry.

This situation could easily be remedied if they rose thirty minutes earlier, and left in plenty of time to get to the meeting, but no, they dilly-dally over

…ıtal trifles until there is a wild rush which enables them to get …ıeeting in time to be late as usual! Some years ago, a brother, at the …onclusion of the Lord's supper, gave out that beautiful hymn by Horatius Bonar, which commences: "Here, O our Lord, we see Thee face to face." He then made a brief comment on the third verse which begins: "Too soon we rise," and suggested that, with some, they would have to alter the words to: "Too late we come!" Another brother altered the verse as follows:

If late we come, when, with some thought and care,
We might have been on time to sup with Thee;
O Lord, forgive, when next the hour is come,
We would be in our place, Thy face to see!

If these words are used to jolt any such habitual late comer to a realization of his thoughtlessness, irreverence, lack of courtesy and indifference to the comfort and convenience of others, the effort will have been well worth while. It is far better to arrive fifteen minutes earlier than the meeting is due to begin. This will allow time for a period of quiet and reverent meditation which will better fit the believer to appreciate and fulfil the purpose of the gathering: the remembrance of the Lord Jesus.

To Come Spiritually Prepared

This is suggested by the words found in 1 Corinthians 11:28, where we read: "But let a man examine himself, and so let him eat of that bread and drink of that cup." It is no light thing to take one's place at the Lord's supper. Many of those believers in Corinth discovered this to their cost, for Paul wrote: "For this cause many are weak and sickly among you, and many sleep" (or have died). There must, therefore, be proper preparation of heart on the part of each believer if he would partake worthily of the Lord's supper. There should be honest self judgment, and all known sin should be confessed to God and turned from.

Scripture gives a list of the sordid things each Christian must put away if he is to be spiritually fit to observe the Lord's supper. Notice some of these things: "anger, wrath, malice, blasphemy, filthy communications, lying, guile, hypocrisies, envies and all evil speakings (See Col. 3:5-9; 1 Peter 2:1). We are told, "If we would judge ourselves, we should not be judged; but when we are judged, we are chastened of the Lord that we should not be condemned with the world" (vs. 31-32).

If dining with the dignitaries of this world demands the meeting of certain requirements, what shall be said about sitting in the presence of the Lord of glory, whose name is above every name? We must therefore come with prepared hearts if we are to remember Him in a way commensurate with His essential Deity, His holy character and His infinite grace. Only as we are impressed with these things shall we come with humble spirits to adore the One who has made us forever His at such great cost.

Moses was made to realize the majesty of Jehovah as he stood by the side of the burning bush. Isaiah had indelibly impressed upon his heart the glory of the Son of God. Ezekiel learned the same truth as he stood on the banks of the river Chebar, and saw the wondrous vision of the Lord. Daniel also, in the light of the revelation of the Ancient of Days, fell upon his face in humility, as he sensed the excellency, beauty and glory of his God. (See Ex. 3:4-6; Isa. 6:1-8; Ezek. 1:4-28; Dan. 7:9; 8:15-27.)

While the believer is welcome to come into the presence of God by virtue of the Savior's sacrifice and high Priestly ministry, yet he must ever bear in mind the exhortation of God's Word which says: "Let us draw near with a true heart, in full assurance of faith, having our hearts sprinkled from an evil conscience, and our bodies washed with pure water" (Heb. 10:22). A preliminary devotional reading of the Scriptures, a period of quiet meditation, and a time of earnest prayer is a necessary requisite to approaching the remembrance feast, and seeking to worship the One who alone is worthy.

In a recent letter, Mr. Robert A. Laidlaw, of New Zealand, author of the most used booklet, "The Reason Why," commenting on the subject of the Lord's supper, wrote: "With the emblems of the gift of Himself before us, in the loaf and the cup, the Lord's supper could become a weekly presentation of ourselves to Him. We ought to say: 'I cannot speak an unkind, an untrue or angry word this week, because last Lord's day I pressed to them the cup which symbolizes the blood by which I was redeemed and sanctified. I cannot do an unworthy deed with this hand, for last Lord's day I stretched it forth and broke the bread which symbolizes His body given for me. I cannot look with these eyes on some unseemly picture, or read some trashy novel, because last Lord's day I gazed upon the chosen emblems of His sacrifice which makes me His for ever, body, soul, and spirit.' But alas, how easily we drift into a routine and sit around the emblems unmoved, without discerning the Lord's body." (See Rom. 12:1-2.)

To Be Reverent

Needless to say, at this meeting, all lightness should be laid aside, and our "behavior be as becometh godliness" (Titus 2:3). This reverence will even be expressed in the posture of our bodies. It should be hardly necessary to point out that the chewing habit is entirely out of place in a meeting of this character. It will also be seen in the clothing we wear. Surely the Lord's supper is not the place for a slouchy posture, or a prideful display of dress. It has been pointed out that the appropriate dress is that which never calls attention to itself. The women, of course, will have a covering on their heads, in obedience to the plain teaching of the New Testament (1 Cor. 11:1-16). It is hardly necessary to point out that there should be no whispering, or looking around or untoward noise during the service.

Little children who are brought to the Lord's supper, can soon be trained to sit quietly during the meeting. Wise mothers, with very little children, will sit near a door so that if the child begins to cry, it can be quickly and quietly removed, and then brought back when quieted. We have all discovered that a very beautiful and most attractive baby can also become a most disturbing element in a meeting, because of the indifference of its parents to the inconvenience it causes when it cries. Someone has said that crying babies in a meeting should be treated like good resolutions—they should be immediately carried out! Babies do not have to be brought to the meeting, but when they are, they should not be allowed to disturb the gathering.

There is a wonderful word in Psalm 89:6-7, which is most appropriate to the gathering of the Lord's people: "For who in heaven can be compared unto the Lord? Who among the sons of the mighty can be likened unto the Lord? God is greatly to be feared in the assembly of the saints, and to be had in reverence of all them that are about Him." Inasmuch as the One we have come to remember is described as "holy and reverend," so also our behavior should be characterized, not by slavish dread, but by "reverence and godly fear" (Ps. 111:9; Heb. 12:28).

One of the grandest descriptions of the dignity, majesty and glory of God is given to us in Isaiah, where we read: "Thus saith the high and lofty One that inhabiteth eternity, whose name is Holy; I dwell in the high and holy place, with him also that is of a contrite and humble spirit, to revive the spirit of the humble, and to revive the heart of the contrite ones" (Isa. 57:15). Thus, this glorious Person, "Infinite, eternal and unchangeable in His Being, wisdom, power, holiness, justice, goodness and truth," is the One around whom we gather to observe the Lord's supper.

To Concentrate One's Mind on the Object of the Meeting

Concentration of mind and heart is no easy thing, but it is essential if we are to fulfil the purpose Christ had in instituting this memorial supper. There is a real need for each believer to discipline his thoughts, and to refuse to allow them to wander here and there on matters that have no connection with the purpose of the gathering. There is no royal road to concentration: it can only come through concentration! The Person, the work and the words of the Lord Jesus will provide plenty of material for our thoughts. We have already suggested some of the things we should remember under the heading of "The purpose of the Lord's supper."

It may be recalled that, in the description of Aaron's garments of glory and beauty, it is said of the mitre: "It shall be upon Aaron's forehead, that Aaron may bear the iniquity of the holy things (Ex. 28:36-38). It is difficult for us to understand how there could be "iniquity" associated with "holy things." It will be observed that the mitre was placed on Aaron's forehead, the seat of his thoughts. How often it is that, in our holiest moments, the flesh will intrude, and God-dishonoring thoughts will come to distract our minds. What is the believer to do under such circumstances? He must bring back his thoughts, by a deliberate effort of the will, to the purpose for which he is there, the remembrance of the Lord Jesus.

An aid to concentration is to think of the words of the hymns that are announced, and to make the language of the hymn the expression of our hearts as we sing them. The same should be true of the spoken words of praise and worship. We should follow intently what the person is saying, for he is speaking on behalf of the whole assembly. Our "Amen," at the conclusion, indicates it is the expression of each one present. We should also give our undivided attention to any Scripture portion that is read, so that we can intelligently follow the train of thought which the reader had in mind when selecting it.

We have all discovered that it is easy to become occupied with some other person in the gathering, and thus lose sight of the One in whose name we have met. Therefore each Christian must constantly challenge himself as his mind begins to wander, and he must seek, by all the means in his power, to bring "into captivity every thought to the obedience of Christ" (2 Cor. 10:5). The purpose of the indwelling Holy Spirit is to occupy the believer's heart and mind with Christ. Therefore, the need to live in the energy of an ungrieved Spirit that He may do His blessed work, unhindered by any tolerated sin or disobedience in our lives.

As the believer sits in the presence of the Lord at His supper, and concentrates his attention and affection upon the altogether lovely One, he will be enabled to sing, in sincerity and truth:

Occupied with Thee, Lord Jesus,
In Thy grace;
All Thy ways and thoughts about me
Only trace
Deeper stories of the glories
Of Thy grace.

Taken up with Thee, Lord Jesus,
I would be;
Finding joy and satisfaction
All in Thee;
Thou the nearest and the dearest
Unto me.

(Miss C. A. Wellesley)

Chapter Twenty-One

The Christian's Responsibility to the Lord's Supper: Join in Praise and Worship

We have elsewhere emphasized the fact that all Christians are priests unto God and, as such, are exhorted to offer up spiritual sacrifices, acceptable to God by Jesus Christ" (1 Peter 2:5). We are further enjoined to offer "the sacrifice of praise to God continually, that is, the fruit of our lips, giving thanks to His name" (Heb. 13:15). This should be particularly true of such a meeting as the Lord's supper. Each Christian should go to that meeting prepared to offer his tribute of praise to the Lord, whether audibly or inaudibly.

God's word to His ancient people was: "Let none appear before Me empty" (Ex. 23:15). He particularly instructed His people that when they came into the land of promise, they should take a selection of their first fruits, place them in a basket, and then present that basket before the Lord and worship Him. (See Deut. 26.) This surely has a voice for us. That basket could be likened to each Christian's heart. As the believer comes to the Lord's supper his heart should be filled with praise and adoration. As each presents his basket, what a volume of worship shall rise from that assembly to the Father and the Son, in the power of the blessed Holy Spirit!

In some assemblies there are certain brethren who have never taken audible part at the Lord's supper. They have never announced a hymn to be sung, never read a portion from the Word, and never led the assembly in praise and worship. Year after year passes by, and their voices are never heard. True, they come to the meeting, and come on time, but if all the brethren followed their example there would be no meeting! Try to imagine, if you can, a Lord's day when, for some unknown reason, only these "silent brethren" happened to be present. Who would give out a hymn? No one. Who would rise to express the praise and worship of the saints? No one. Who would give thanks for the bread and the cup? No one! Thus there would be no meeting.

This silence may stem from various causes. It may be due to an understandable timidity and the fear of hearing their own voice in a gathering of Christians. It is perfectly true that some believers are naturally bolder than others, yet this natural reluctance must be honestly faced in the presence of God, and right action taken in regard to it. It is good to recall David's words: "I sought the Lord, and He heard me, and delivered me from all my fears" (Ps. 34:4). Many a person has allowed himself to be gagged because of the fear of what men might say or think of him. It is still true that "the fear of man bringeth a snare" (Prov. 29:35).

If this is being read by one of these silent brethren, let this encourage him to take part audibly. Should the Lord lay upon your heart an appropriate hymn, in keeping with the theme of the meeting, why not rise and announce the number of that hymn and then sit down. There is no need to read the first verse, and no need whatever to read the whole hymn. In this way the ice will be broken, and it will be easier next time.

It is heart warming to hear a number of the brethren, and particularly the younger brethren, rise one after the other, without a hymn between, and give a short expression of their appreciation of the Lord Jesus, each in his own way. This brings great delight to God, joy to their own souls and edification to the whole assembly.

Then again, the silence on the part of this brother may be due to a failure to realize his solemn responsibility in a meeting of this character. It was the idea of letting the more gifted men do all the speaking that opened the way for the introduction of clerisy many years ago, and this has wrought untold mischief. How do people become gifted? By exercising the gift that God has given them. In so doing, they developed their gift. All doubtless began to speak in fear and with much trembling, but they gradually acquired, through practice, an improved facility to express their thoughts. No one will develop the gift of speaking by remaining silent!

Each believer, then, should honestly and prayerfully face his responsibilities in this direction and be prepared, if the Lord so leads, to make his vocal contribution to the praise and worship of the assembly. Remember, it is not the mere eloquence of the words spoken, but the spiritual sincerity of the speaker that counts with God. A few simple words, spoken from the heart, is of far more value than the most eloquent expression of praise and ministry.

Perhaps the silent brother may have nothing to say because he has not been listening to God. He may have failed to maintain his daily devotional reading and meditation in the Word of God. He may have become slack in the matter of prayer, or in his daily witness for Christ to others. The only remedy for this is an honest confession of this fact to God, and a holy determination to return to that Bible study, prayer and praise. As he does so, he will discover, as David did: "My heart was hot within me, while I was musing the fire burned: then spake I with my tongue" (Ps. 39:3).

Sometimes, at a social gathering of the same company of believers, these "silent brethren" can wax very eloquent, and hold forth at considerable length on any topic in which they are *really* interested. The moral is surely obvious. Only as they are *interested* in spiritual things will they speak of them. Our Lord pointed out that: "Out of the abundance of the heart the mouth speaketh" (Matt. 12:34). Once the heart is filled with Christ, the mouth will give evidence of that fact.

It may be that this habitually silent brother has been careless in his Christian life during the week. One thing is certain: carelessness and worldliness of life, from Monday to Saturday, is not productive of spiritual exercise on the Lord's day. As we mentioned earlier, a person cannot bury the spirit of worship six days a week, and then expect a resurrection on Sunday. The high cost of spirituality is exceeded only by the *higher cost* of unspirituality! There must be a resolute turning away from all worldliness and compromise in the life, if each believer is to make his contribution to the spirituality of the whole assembly. This is the day of the multiplicity of secular magazines, some good, others indifferent and quite a number that are positively bad, yet all possess the same fatal tendency to keep the child of God from the study of the holy Scriptures. Often far more time is spent reading the newspaper than the Book of books.

Once more, it may be the failure of this silent brother to become acquainted with the contents of the hymn book used at the Lord's supper. In this book there is a collection of beautiful hymns, in choice language, eminently suited to express the praise and worship of the Lord's people as they meet to remember their Lord. Some of these hymns were written hundreds of years ago, others are of more recent date, but all are redolent with Christ and His many glories. The pity is that so few of the hymns are sung. Very often the same hymns are sung over and over again, and some very beautiful hymns are never sung at all. It would be a helpful exercise if every believer bought a copy of the hymn book, and read at least one hymn a day during his private devotions. In this way his mind would become a veritable treasure house of choice expressions of praise.

While on the subject of hymns, perhaps it may be well to point out the very useful purpose they serve. In the early days of the Church there were no hymn books such as we have today. We find, however, that these gatherings of believers were accompanied by "psalms, hymns and spiritual songs" (Eph. 5:19). The early Jewish converts brought with them the psalmody of the synagogues, for they had a wonderful collection of hymns in the Psalms of David, "the sweet singer of Israel." In Corinth the Greek custom of rhapsodizing, or extempore cantillation, was brought into the assembly. It was this that called forth the statement: "Every one of you hath a psalm" (or hymn). Paul did not criticise them for this custom, but sought to regulate its proper use so as to eliminate any confusion (1 Cor. 14:26). Thus the singing of psalms and hymns played no small part in the assemblies of the early Christians.

Today we have, in our hymnbooks, a beautiful collection of poems by which to express our praise and worship. These hymns are true to the Word and honoring to Christ, and are well calculated to lead out our hearts in true worship at the Lord's supper. These hymns are set to appropriate tunes and, in the case of some hymn books, the words are inserted *between the lines of the music*, that all can follow the correct time and tune indicated in the music. Such a hymn book is *Hymns of Worship and Remembrance*, which contains 350 hymns, properly classified as to their subject matter. This is published by Truth and Praise, Inc. (available from ECS Ministries). It is an excellent collection of scriptural and spiritual hymns for the Lord's people at such gatherings, and is warmly recommended for use in the assemblies of the Lord's people.

Like all good things, however, hymns can be both a boon and a bane. A boon if they are used rightly, and a bane if they are allowed to crowd out the spontaneous oral worship of the Lord's people. There is an old truism which affirms that "the abuse of the best is the worst." The Lord's supper does not exist merely for the purpose of singing hymns, but also provides an opportunity for several of the brethren to take part orally in praise and worship. The temptation is to use the hymn book as a *substitute* for the spoken expressions of praise, or the reading of the Scriptures. Thus the Lord's supper is sometimes allowed to become a mere service of song. True, the hymns that are sung are good. but the meeting should not be allowed to be confined to this form of praise.

The story is told of a young Christian, recently saved from heathenism, who visited England. While in that country, he attended many meetings for the breaking of bread. On his return to his own country he described his impressions of this meeting somewhat as follows: "I noticed that in this meeting two black books were used. One of them was small (the hymn book), and the other was large (the Bible). During the meeting the little black book was opened many times and each time the people sang from it; but the big black book was very seldom opened and, in some of the meetings, it was never opened at all." Though he knew it not, this young Christian indicated the danger we have in mind, namely: that the hymn book may be allowed to supersede the Bible, or become a substitute for the spoken expressions of worship from the saints.

It must ever be kept in mind that the hymn book is not a substitute for, but merely an adjunct to the spiritual worship of believers. The Lord's supper should never be allowed to degenerate into a song festival, even though the hymns have been penned by spiritually gifted Christians. It requires far more spiritual exercise for a brother to rise and audibly express, in his own words, the praise and worship of an assembly, than to merely announce a hymn which does it for him. We must ever be on our guard against the tendency of the flesh to use hymns as a kind of stop gap, or a means to cover up our spiritual barrenness. It would be far better to have no hymns at all, than to allow the hymn book to rob believers of that essential spiritual preparation, by which they are enabled orally to express the worship of the assembly.

There is also the tendency for a worship meeting to become sterotyped, and to follow a sameness of pattern, such as a succession of a hymn and a prayer, a hymn and a prayer, right through the entire meeting. Not that this is wrong, but to adopt and maintain it as a *pattern* to be slavishly followed, does not commend itself as being indicative of the liberty of the Spirit. Most meetings for the observance of the Lord's supper would be far better with fewer hymns and more spoken expressions of worship.

The question of guidance as to when to take audible part at the Lord's supper is not easy to answer, There are two extremes to be avoided. One is to rush ahead of God, and the other is to lag behind. These two extremes are referred to in Psalm 32:9, where we read: "Be not as the horse or as the mule, which have no understanding: whose mouth must be held in with bit and bridle, lest they come near unto thee." The horse is noted for its *spirited impetuousity*, rushing heedless into the battle. The mule is famous for its *stubborn inertia*, refusing to budge when commanded to go. The remedy is found in Ps. 32:8, where God says: "I will instruct thee and teach thee in the way that thou shalt go: I will guide thee with Mine eye" ["I will counsel thee. Mine eye shall be upon thee." marg.]

We must beware of obeying any impulse that comes into our minds, for this may only be due to the impatience of the flesh. It is only as we come spiritually prepared that God will impress our hearts as to whether we should give out a hymn, or express the praise and worship of the assembly, or read a portion from the Word, or pass on a word of ministry. The Holy Spirit delights to occupy the believer with the Person of Christ, and as He is allowed to lead, He will do His blessed work and guide us into all truth. It cannot be overemphasized that scriptural principles of gathering must be accompanied by spiritual power for their operation. Where this is absent, there will only be a cold formalism and banal, empty phraseology, characterized by a number of outworn cliches which do not produce any spiritual grip upon the souls of those who are present.

A lovely illustration of the effect of unity of heart and voice, in praise and worship, is seen at the dedication of the Temple in Jerusalem. We are told: "It came to pass, as the trumpeters and singers were as one, to make one sound to be heard in praising and thanking the Lord; and when they lifted up their voice with the trumpets and cymbals and instruments of music, and praised the Lord saying: 'For He is good; for His mercy endureth for ever! that then the house was filled with a cloud, even the house of the Lord" (2 Chron. 5:13). Doubtless it was this incident that prompted the hymn that begins:

Lord Jesus Christ, we seek Thy face,
Within the veil we bow the knee;
O, let Thy glory fill the place,
And bless us while we wait on Thee.
(A. Stewart)

There is no meeting comparable to the observance of the Lord's supper, when it is conducted along scriptural lines, and observed by spiritual believers. As they come, with prepared hearts, in humble dependence upon the Lord Jesus and the guidance of the Holy Spirit of God, there will rise from their hearts a volume of praise and worship which shall delight the One whose supper it is. This, in turn, will bring joy and blessing to those who thus seek to remember the Lord Jesus in the way that He instructed His people to do on the eve of Calvary. May we know much of His divine guidance as we seek to remember Him!

Chapter Twenty-Two

A Summary of the Lord's Supper

It may be profitable to summarize, in a few words, what has been said more fully in the preceding pages. The Lord's supper is:

A Place of Glad Obedience

The observance of it is an act of obedience to the Lord Jesus, who instituted it on the night of His cruel betrayal, and who said to His disciples: "This do for a remembrance of Me." Years after, He gave a special revelation to His servant Paul, and again repeated His request: "This do for a remembrance of Me." Thus it is in obedience to the Lord's own request that His people gather to observe this ordinance.

A Place of Expressed Unity

It is a coming together, in fellowship, of those who have been united to the Lord Jesus as members of His mystical body, the Church. This unity is manifested as, with one heart and voice, they join to praise and adore the Son of God.

A Place of Scriptural Simplicity

All that is required is a loaf of bread and a cup containing the fruit of the vine. No provision whatever is made in the New Testament for an officiating minister, an ornate ritual, or a prescribed order of service, or a prayer book and, least of all, for gorgeous vestments. Any two or three believers, meeting in the name that is above every name, may take the bread and the cup in fond memory of the One, "whom, having not seen, they love."

A Place of Acknowledged Lordship

It is at the Lord's supper that the Lordship of Christ is paramount. Therefore, no one should attempt to take His place as the Host at His own supper. The promise of His presence: "There am I in the midst," is all that Christians need. It is He alone who gives virtue and value to this meeting.

A Place of Personal Heart Preparation

The believer is urged to examine himself in the light of God's presence ere he comes to the supper. There must be honest self judgment, confession of all known sin, and a turning away from all that would hinder him from worshipping in Spirit and in truth.

A Place of Humble Dependence

The Christian still has the flesh within him, which ardently longs for self expression and self exaltation. He therefore needs to be dependent on the indwelling Holy Spirit to lead him into all truth, and empower him to worthily accomplish the highest of all occupations—the worship of the Father and the Son.

A Place of Exercised Priesthood

Each believer is a priest and, as such, is urged to "offer up spiritual sacrifices, acceptable to God by Jesus Christ" (1 Peter 2:5-10). Every Christian should therefore be exercised before the Lord, so that each may offer true praise and worship, either audibly or inaudibly.

A Place of Glad Submission

The Word of God is our sole authority, both for faith and practice. Each believer should therefore unhesitatingly submit to what it clearly teaches (1 Cor. 14:37). The women should have their heads covered and be silent in the assembly, simply because this is what the Bible clearly teaches (1 Cor. 11:1-16; 14:34).

A Place of Grateful Remembrance

The sole purpose of the Lord's supper is to remember the Person of the Lord Jesus. Thus each Christian should focus his attention and affection on the Son of God, who loved him and gave Himself for him. As he does this, there will flow up, from his heart, true gratitude and reverent worship to his Savior and Lord, which will bring pleasure to the Lord Jesus.

A Place of Adoring Worship

Prayer occupies us with our needs; praise with our blessings; but worship occupies us with the Lord Himself, to the exclusion of all else. Worship is the ascription of worth to One who is worthy, and this will be the occupation of all the redeemed in eternity. As the believer seeks to remember his Lord and Savior, at the Lord's supper, there will be an ever increasing appreciation of the Person of Christ, as He gives him new unfoldings of His many glories. At such a meeting there should rise, from every heart, without one discordant note, songs of praise to the Lamb that was slain and that liveth again!

A Place of Spiritual Discernment

As each Christian takes the bread and drinks the cup, he should spiritually discern the Lord's body and His precious blood. True, they are only symbols, but they are the symbols of that by which his eternal redemption has been secured. Thus he spiritually apprehends this glorious fact as he partakes of the elements, and worships the One who, at such infinite cost, has made him forever His.

A Place of Hallowed Privilege

Who can possibly fully appreciate the high honor conferred upon sinners, saved by grace, to be enabled to sit in the presence of the King of kings and Lord of lords, and enter into the holiest by virtue of that precious blood of their Redeemer! If dining with the worldly great is considered a privilege, what shall be said of the person who sits in the presence of the One who is described as "the King eternal, immortal, invisible, the only wise God" to whom "be honor and glory for ever and ever" (1 Tim. 1:17).

A Place of Confident Proclamation

By the observance of the Lord's death, the greatest event in the history of the universe, the event to which an eternal past looked forward, and to which an eternal future shall look backward. That event is "The center of two eternities which look, with rapt, adoring eyes, backward and on to thee."

A Place of Joyous Anticipation

The Lord's supper is only to be observed "Till He come." Each Lord's day the believer is reminded of the promise of his Lord to return to take His blood-bought people to the home He has prepared for them. For all eternity they shall not only be with Him, but they shall be like Him and praise Him for the matchless grace that led Him, though rich, for our sakes to become poor that we, through His poverty, might be made rich (2 Cor. 8:9).

The second coming of the Lord Jesus is the great event to which every believer looks forward with glad expectation.

> If here on earth the thoughts of Jesus' love
> Lift our poor hearts this weary world above,
> If even here the taste of heavenly springs
> So cheers the spirit that the pilgrim sings,
> What will the sunshine of His glory prove?
> What the unmingled fulness of His love?
> What hallelujahs shall His presence raise?
> What, but one loud eternal burst of praise?
>
> (J. G. Deck)

May it be ours, as we wait for "the glorious appearing of our great God and Savior Jesus Christ," not only to live for His praise and glory, witness to others of His saving grace and power, and loyally serve Him, motivated by His constraining love; but also, each Lord's day, count it the greatest honor and privilege of our lives to gather with our fellow believers at the Lord's supper, and remember the One who remembered us in our deep need and gave Himself for us.

May these pages be used by the Lord to impress the hearts of all Christians everywhere with the importance of this blessed ordinance! May He lead many, not only to see their privilege of partaking of the Lord's supper each Lord's day; but also to take their place with those who gather in scriptural simplicity, to fulfil the request of the Lord Jesus, "This do for a remembrance of Me."